# HAVE YOUR SAY!

Manual on the revised European Charter
on the Participation of Young People
in Local and Regional Life

Council of Europe Publishing

*The opinions expressed in this work are the responsibility of the author(s) and do not necessarily reflect the official policy of the Council of Europe.*

All rights reserved. No part of this publication may be translated, reproduced or transmitted, in any form or by any means, electronic (CD-Rom, Internet, etc.) or mechanical, including photocopying, recording or any information storage or retrieval system, without prior permission in writing from the Public Information and Publications Division, Directorate of Communication (F-67075 Strasbourg Cedex or publishing@coe.int).

Youth Department
Directorate of Democratic Citizenship and Participation
Council of Europe
F-67075 Strasbourg Cedex
Tel.: +33 (0)3 88 41 23 00
Fax: +33 (0)3 88 41 27 77
e-mail: youth@coe.int
www.coe.int/youth

Cover design: Graphic Design Workshop, Council of Europe
Layout: Jouve, Paris

Council of Europe Publishing
F-67075 Strasbourg Cedex
http://book.coe.int

ISBN 978-92-871-8165-7
© Council of Europe, November 2015
Printed at the Council of Europe

# Table of contents

**ACKNOWLEDGEMENTS** .................................................. 5

**PREFACE** .................................................. 7

**INTRODUCTION** .................................................. 9

**CHAPTER 1: INTRODUCTION TO PARTICIPATION**
    1.1. Basic definitions and approaches to youth participation .................................................. 11
    1.2. Benefits of and barriers to youth participation .................................................. 16
    1.3. Principles of youth participation .................................................. 20
    1.4. Preconditions for youth participation .................................................. 23
    1.5. Forms of youth participation .................................................. 25

**CHAPTER 2: THE REVISED EUROPEAN CHARTER ON THE PARTICIPATION OF YOUNG PEOPLE IN LOCAL AND REGIONAL LIFE**
    2.1. Introduction .................................................. 27
    2.2. Content of the charter .................................................. 31
    2.3. Target groups of the charter .................................................. 35

**CHAPTER 3: THE CHARTER'S APPROACH TO PARTICIPATION**
    3.1. Introduction to the charter's approach to youth participation .................................................. 37
    3.2. RMSOS framework .................................................. 38

**CHAPTER 4: THE CHARTER IN PRACTICE**
    4.1. The revised charter as a practical tool for different actors .................................................. 45
    4.2. How to use the charter in practice? .................................................. 51
        a. The six-step-model .................................................. 51
        b. RMSOS approach .................................................. 53
        c. Participatory approach to planning youth projects .................................................. 53

**CHAPTER 5: YOUTH PARTICIPATION PROJECTS**
    5.1. Managing youth participation projects ............................................. 55
    5.2. Step-by-step: planning and managing a youth project ........................... 57
    5.3. Quality criteria for participatory projects .......................................... 64

**CHAPTER 6: CO-OPERATION AT A LOCAL LEVEL**
    6.1. Getting ready for co-operation ..................................................... 69
    6.2. Co-operation in the area of decision-making – Consultation model ............ 71
    6.3. Co-operation in the area of decision-making – Committee model .............. 76
    6.4. Co-operation in the area of decision-making – Co-management ............... 79
    6.5. Other forms of co-operation in the area of decision-making .................... 83

**CHAPTER 7: THE CHARTER AND LOCAL YOUTH POLICIES**
    7.1. Introduction to local youth policy .................................................. 85
    7.2. The revised charter and local youth policy ....................................... 88
    7.3. Formulation process of a local youth policy ...................................... 92
    7.4. Advocacy – network for policy change ............................................ 94

**CHAPTER 8: EDUCATIONAL SECTION**
    Diamond of policies ....................................................................100
    Human sandwiches .....................................................................102
    Knives and forks ........................................................................103
    Ladder of participation .................................................................106
    Meeting the mayor .....................................................................109
    Participation grid .......................................................................112
    Participation snowball .................................................................113
    Participation timeline ..................................................................115
    Rights and participation ...............................................................116
    RMSOS charades .......................................................................117
    Role play on the charter ................................................................118
    Statement exercise .....................................................................121
    The triangle of co-operation ..........................................................123
    True or false? ............................................................................126
    What can you do for me? ..............................................................128
    Visit to Jeunessia .......................................................................129
    What happens if it doesn't happen? .................................................130
    Simulation exercise "Youth in action" ...............................................131

**BIBLIOGRAPHY** ..............................................................................139

**CONTACTS** ..................................................................................141

# Acknowledgements

This manual was written by Żaneta Goździk-Ormel.

It was produced under the guidance and support of a reference group composed of:

Sunduss Al-Hassani
Dietrich Baenziger
Iris Bawidamann
James Doorley
Viktoria Kharchenko
Nadine Lyamouri-Bajja
With acknowledgements to Giusepinna Rossi for the pictograms.

# Preface

The aim of the Council of Europe's youth policy is to provide young people with equal opportunities and experience which enable them to develop the knowledge, skills and competencies to play a full part in all aspects of society. The programme of the European Youth Centres in Budapest and in Strasbourg and the projects supported by the European Youth Foundation are living examples of the involvement of young people in exercising their rights and responsibilities as citizens. It is often at the local level – in schools, youth and cultural centres, in local youth councils, in participative budget projects, in sports and cultural projects, that youth participation is meaningful to the lives of most young people.

The Congress of Local and Regional Authorities, the political assembly of elected representatives from the grassroots levels of the Council of Europe member States, is deeply committed to fostering greater participation of young people in the democratic structures and processes of our societies, particularly at the levels at which its representatives undertake their work.

Through its work to find responses to the challenges of modern society, the Congress issues policy recommendations and encourages local and regional authorities to implement them. If these policies are to be successful and meet the needs of all citizens, the Congress firmly believes that citizens, especially young people, should be actively involved in the decision and policy-making processes. It is precisely at the local and regional levels that a culture of citizen participation can most effectively take root.

The Congress supports the Council of Europe's system of co-management, in line with the decision-making principles developed and espoused by its youth sector in its forty-odd years of existence. This system, which involves the collective taking of decisions on all issues by public authorities in partnership with youth representatives and their organisations, takes young people, their concerns and their ability to take decisions and accept responsibility seriously. It is through co-management systems that young people can best be encouraged to engage with the authorities and in society. This is of particular importance at a time when research shows young people are increasingly rejecting traditional methods to have their say.

The Revised European Charter on the Participation of Young People in Local and Regional Life is the key instrument in promoting co-management at regional and local levels. Indeed it was itself produced by a group of young people and local and regional authority representatives working in equal partnership. The Charter is aimed principally at local and regional authorities and is a guide to implementing sectoral policies that will benefit both young people and other citizens.

It is also a tool that young people can use to encourage local and regional authorities to implement policies in full consultation with them, as well as for co-operation between young people, youth organisations, and local and regional authorities.

Young people must have the right, means, space, opportunity and support to participate in decision and policy making. The aim of the Charter is to promote this process. There are many examples to illustrate the importance of meaningful youth participation at local and regional levels, but much work still needs to be done to achieve this goal throughout Europe, and the manual "Have Your Say!" will no doubt serve to further this process.

The first edition of this manual has been one of the most successful publications of the Council of Europe youth sector. This bears witness to the fact that Europe is moving forward and increasingly accepting the importance of citizen participation. This manual is an important and valuable tool in this process, and we invite everyone, and especially local and regional authorities, to use it to promote a society which better reflects young people's needs throughout Europe.

Andreas Kiefer

Secretary General
Congress of Local and
Regional Authorities of the
Council of Europe

Snežana Samardžić-Marković

Director General
Directorate General of
Democracy of the
Council of Europe

# Introduction

Welcome to *Have Your Say! – a manual on the revised European Charter on the Participation of Young People in Local and Regional Life.*

Youth participation is not an end in itself, but a means of achieving positive changes in young people's lives and of building a better society. In recent years, there have been a growing number of initiatives promoting and strengthening youth involvement at very different levels – international, regional, national and local. New tools have also been created for those working in this area. One such tool is the revised European Charter on the Participation of Young People in Local and Regional Life (hereinafter referred to as the Charter), adopted in May 2003 by the Congress of Local and Regional Authorities of the Council of Europe.[1]

Participation of young people was also one of the three main themes of the European Youth Campaign for Diversity, Human Rights and Participation, organised by the Council of Europe, in partnership with the European Commission and the European Youth Forum (2006/2007). This manual is one of the initiatives undertaken in the framework of this campaign.

The revised charter is designed as a tool to support young people, youth workers, organisations and local authorities in promoting and enhancing meaningful youth participation at local level across Europe and it may be used in a variety of different ways. Some users might be able to implement it immediately, while others might need support in order to learn how to make the best use of the revised charter in their own environment. The questions: "What do I do with the charter?"; "How do I use it in practice?" or "Why should I be interested in this document?", have often been asked by those working in youth participation at local level. The aim of this manual is to help find the right answers for different European contexts.

The manual is not a ready-to-use guide on how to implement the charter at a local level – the situation varies enormously throughout Europe. It is rather a collection of reflections and questions that can help those working at local level to find their own ways of achieving meaningful participation by young people. The publication is divided into eight chapters, each of them focusing on a different aspect related to youth participation and the charter itself.

Chapter 1 provides a basic introduction to youth participation by presenting definitions, principles and factors influencing participation. Chapter 2 contains details about the charter, its content and target groups and also some background information about the Congress of Local and Regional Authorities of the Council of Europe. Chapter 3 explains the charter's approach to youth participation, which is based on the five key words – right, means, space, opportunity and support. Chapter 4 presents possible ways of using the charter in practice,

---

1. The name of the Congress of Local and Regional Authorities of Europe was changed on 14 October 2003 to the Congress of Local and Regional Authorities of the Council of Europe. The latter will be used throughout this publication.

focusing on a step-by-step approach that can be used at a local level. Youth projects play a very important role in promoting and strengthening youth participation and Chapter 5 looks at issues related to organising a youth project. The charter can be best used if local actors interested in youth participation co-operate and work in partnership. Thus, Chapter 6 provides ideas on how to develop good co-operation at a local level, especially between youth organisations and local authorities. The charter can also be seen as a tool for the creation of local youth policy, and Chapter 7 explains how this document can be used to formulate or to review youth policies at community or regional level. Finally, Chapter 8 presents a number of educational activities that can be used as learning aids related to youth participation and especially to the revised charter. In addition, each chapter contains sections called "reflection time". These are a collection of questions that can help a reader to discover the best ways of using the charter in his/her own context.

This manual is the result of co-operation between the Directorate of Youth and Sport (DYS) and the Congress which started many years ago. Indeed, the foundation for what was to become the European Charter on the Participation of Young People in Local and Regional Life was laid at the first and second conference on youth policies, organised by the then Standing Conference of Local and Regional Authorities of Europe, in Lausanne (June 1988) and in Llangollen (September 1991) respectively. The revised charter, to which this manual is a companion, resulted from a conference to celebrate the tenth anniversary of the original 1992 charter. This conference, entitled "Young People – Actors in their Towns and Regions", was organised by the Congress, in partnership with the DYS, in Cracow, Poland, on 7 and 8 March 2002. Apart from evaluating progress made in the field of youth participation during the charter's ten years of existence, the participants furthermore called for a revision of the charter, in order to take account of new challenges faced by young people in contemporary society. Since the adoption of the revised charter, the Congress and the DYS have co-operated on initiatives to promote its implementation; the Congress itself continues to work on issues of concern to young people, at local and regional levels, through its various structures and texts.

This manual could not have been created without the contribution of several individuals. Special thanks are due to Żaneta Goździk-Ormel, for her dedicated work as the manual's author. Words of thanks are also owed to the reference group for their involvement, support and advice.

# Chapter 1
## introduction to participation

### 1.1. Basic definitions and approaches to youth participation

When dealing with youth participation, one can observe a variety of practices as well as a diversity of approaches and theories. Youth workers, youth organisations and local authorities approach the concept of participation from different angles due to the diversity of their backgrounds and experience. The motivation behind their work in the area of youth participation is often very different too: some may be motivated by social change and the building of more democratic societies; while others may be interested in the development of young people or may simply be motivated by their own political aims. The debate related to different aspects of youth participation is an ongoing one and various answers can be given to the same questions.

> *Reflection time*
> 1. How does your community/organisation define youth (age limit, psychological criteria or other criteria)?
> 2. Who are the young people you work with? To what extent are they a homogenous group?
> 3. How is "youth participation" understood in your organisation/institution?
> 4. How do you know this? Is there an agreed definition/approach or rather your own assumption and perception?
> 5. What does your organisation want to achieve in the area of youth participation?

If answers to the above questions were collected from youth workers, leaders, authorities' representatives or other people interested in youth participation throughout Europe, the result would probably be as many ideas as persons asked. It is not realistic to expect that it is possible to create one definition or approach, agreed on by everybody. Here are a few examples of how some organisations or groups understand youth participation:

– "In a nutshell participation means to be involved, to have tasks and to share and take over responsibility. It means to have access and to be included."[2]

---
2. Lauritzen, P., keynote speech on participation presented at the Training Course on the development and implementation of participation projects at local and regional level, the European Youth Centre, Strasbourg, June 2006.

- Participation means "helping to steer and to form".[3]
- "Participation is about talking and listening, expressing your own views and listening while others express theirs. It can mean working together for a solution or a course of action. Participating doesn't just mean becoming a young activist, it can also mean taking advantage of opportunities that are being offered, like joining clubs to learn a new skill, or groups that feel strongly about an issue."[4]

> *Reflection time*
>
> 1. *What are the similarities between your understanding of youth participation and the definitions presented above?*
> 2. *What are the main differences?*

For the purpose of this manual, youth participation will be understood as defined in the preamble of the revised European Charter on the Participation of Young People in Local and Regional Life:[5]

"Participation in the democratic life of any community is about more than voting or standing for election, although these are important elements. Participation and active citizenship is about having the right, the means, the space and the opportunity and where necessary the support to participate in and influence decisions and engaging in actions and activities so as to contribute to building a better society."

The above definition goes beyond a narrow understanding of youth participation solely as political involvement or participation in youth councils. It stresses that to participate means having influence on and responsibility for decisions and actions that affect the lives of young people or are simply important to them. In practice, therefore, this could mean voting in local elections as well as setting up a youth organisation or an Internet forum to exchange information about hobbies and interests or other creative ways of spending free time. The charter's definition of participation also shows a shift in the approach to young people and youth involvement. Young people are not treated as victims or as a vulnerable group that needs protection and help (the so-called "problem-based approach"). They are not treated as objects of adults' intervention, with the adults assuming that they know what is best for young people. Young people are now seen as active players in organisations or in community life; they are seen as partners with lots of potential, talents and strengths. They should have the opportunity to express their needs and to find ways of satisfying them. An African proverb says "the one wearing the shoes knows exactly where they hurt". That is why young people must be involved in dealing with issues that affect them and why they should be supported by others rather than instructed by them.

---

3. Jans, M. and De Backer, K., *Youth and social participation. Elements for a practical theory*, Flemish Youth Council JeP!, Brussels, 2002, p. 2.
4. *Discussing global issues: what is participation?* UNICEF, United Kingdom, 2004, p. 1.
5. *The revised European Charter on the Participation of Young People in Local and Regional Life,* Congress of Local and Regional Authorities of the Council of Europe, May 2003.

> *Reflection time*
>
> 1. Are young people in your community/organisation seen:
>    - as a group that needs to have its problems solved by somebody else?
>    - as a group not wanting to take responsibility?
>    - as a group that needs protection?
>    - as clients that need to have everything provided?
>    - as persons having strengths and talents?
>    - as a group that is capable of contributing to the solving of their own problems?
>    - as a group that wants to do things by itself (not accepting help)?
>    - in any other way?
> 2. Is there anything that needs to be changed in the way young people are perceived in your community/organisation? If so, what?

In the last decade youth participation has often been referred to as a right (the so-called "rights approach" to youth participation). UNICEF, for example, sees participation as a human right and therefore the UN Convention of the Rights of the Child underlines children's right to participate. Roger Hart (author of the concept called the "ladder of participation") says that participation is a fundamental right of citizenship because it is a way of learning what it means to be a citizen. In the Council of Europe, youth participation is perceived as "the right of young people to be included and to assume duties and responsibilities in daily life at local level as well as the right to influence the processes of their lives democratically".[6] Participation being a right also means that all young people can exercise this right without discrimination – no matter where they come from or what language they speak.

Youth participation can also be seen as a form of a youth-adult partnership. "Partnership is about doing things together. It is about listening to everyone's voice and taking different ideas seriously"[7]. In practice this means that aims, objectives, roles, responsibilities, decisions, etc., are negotiated and agreed upon, and that young people and adults know precisely:

- where they are going;
- what is expected of them;
- what they expect of others;
- how they are going to do this;
- what kind of support they are getting and from where.

The advantage of youth-adult partnership is that it brings together the skills and talents of young people and the experience and wisdom of adults. It also ensures that all individual contributions are recognised and valued, thereby motivating the partners to undertake more initiatives and projects.

---

6. Boukobza, E., *Keys to participation. A practitioners' guide*, Council of Europe, 1998, p. 10.
7. Stacey, K., "Theoretical underpinnings of youth partnership accountability", unpublished paper, Adelaide, 1998; quoted in *Youth participation handbook for organizations. A guide for organizations seeking to involve young people on boards and committees,* Government of South Australia Office for Youth, 2003, p. 15.

> *Reflection time*
>
> *Look at your organisation or community. Would you say that a partnership between young people and adults already exists there?*
>
> 1. *If yes, what form does it take?*
>
> 2. *If not, why do you think it does not exist? Is there anything that can be done to promote it? What can you do?*

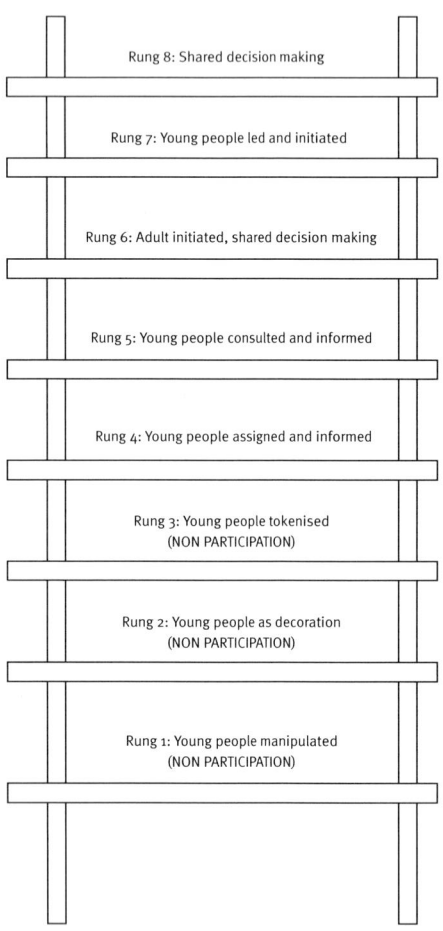

Adapted from: Hart, R., *Children's participation from tokenism to citizenship*, UNICEF Innocenti Research Centre, Florence, 1992

It is not enough to say that young people do or do not participate. There are different degrees to which youth can be involved or can take over responsibility, depending on the local situation, resources, needs and level of experience. Roger Hart proposes a model of the so-called "ladder of children's participation",[8] which illustrates the different degrees of involvement of children and young people in projects, organisations or communities.

Roger Hart defines eight degrees of youth involvement, each of the degrees corresponding to one rung of a ladder:

*Rung 8: Shared decision-making*

Projects or ideas are initiated by young people, who invite the adults to take part in the decision-making process as partners.

*Rung 7: Young people led and initiated*

Projects or ideas are initiated and directed by young people; the adults might get invited to provide any necessary support, but a project can carry on without their intervention.

*Rung 6: Adult-initiated, shared decision making*

Adults initiate projects but young people are invited to share the decision-making power and responsibilities as equal partners.

*Rung 5: Young people consulted and informed*

Projects are initiated and run by adults, but young people provide advice and suggestions and are informed how these suggestions contribute to the final decisions or results.

*Rung 4: Young people assigned and informed*

Projects are initiated and run by adults; young people are invited to take on some specific roles or tasks within the project, but they are aware of what influence they have in reality.

*Rung 3: Young people tokenised (tokenism)*

---

8. Hart, R., *Children's participation from tokenism to citizenship*, UNICEF Innocenti Research Centre, Florence, 1992. This model has been based on S. Arnstein's "ladder of citizen's participation", published as "A ladder of citizen participation", *JAIP*, Vol. 35, No. 4, July 1969, pp. 216-24.

Young people are given some roles within projects but they have no real influence on any decisions. The illusion is created (either on purpose or unintentionally) that young people participate, when in fact they have no choice about what they do and how.

*Rung 2: Young people as decoration*

Young people are needed in the project to represent youth as an underprivileged group. They have no meaningful role (except from being present) and – as happens with any decorations – they are put in a visible position within a project or organisation, so that they can easily be seen by outsiders.

*Rung 1: Young people manipulated*

Young people are invited to take part in the project, but they have no real influence on decisions and their outcomes. In fact, their presence is used to achieve some other goal, such as winning a local election, creating a better impression of an institution or securing some extra funds from institutions that support youth participation.

The ladder of youth participation can be a very useful tool for practitioners, who want to look critically at how participatory projects or initiatives work in their own communities. But this model can also falsely suggest a hierarchy of degrees of youth participation[9] and can encourage efforts to reach the highest rungs at any price. It is therefore important to remember that the degree to which young people are or should be involved depends on the local situation, on what needs to be achieved, what experience exists, etc. It can sometimes be rather difficult to see precisely what the level of participation is within a project, either due to its complexity or to the fact that there are no clear borders between different rungs. The degree of involvement can also evolve over time.

> **Reflection time**
> 1. Where is your project or initiative on the ladder of youth participation?
> 2. How do you know this?
> 3. On which level of the ladder would your project be most effective? Why?
> 4. How can your project reach this level?

When talking about youth participation, one can ask a very legitimate question: "participation in what?" The United Nations General Assembly distinguishes the following areas of youth participation:[10]

- economic participation – relates to employment and work in general, to economic development, eliminating poverty, building a stable economic situation in a society, a region or for young people as a group;
- political participation – relates to authorities and governments, public policies, exercising power, the influence on the distribution of resources at different levels;
- social participation – relates to involvement in the life of a local community, addressing local problems and challenges;
- cultural participation – relates to different forms of art and expression (visual arts, music, film, dance, etc.).

---

9. There are also a few other models of degrees of youth participation, which do not imply a hierarchical structure. Compare, for example, the models of Davis Driskell or Phil Treseder.
10. The United Nations Youth Agenda, *Empowering youth for development and peace* at: www.un.org/esa/socdev/unyin/agenda.htm (last visited on 3 October 2006).

These areas can be interrelated, and sometimes when looking at an initiative or project it becomes clear that this initiative deals with more than one area. It is not easy to say which areas of participation interest young people the most, but research among British youth shows that they are mainly interested in the production and consumption of music, dance and different forms of art, as well as in sporting activities.[11]

> *Reflection time*
>
> 1. *What could be examples of concrete activities or projects within the four above-mentioned areas of participation?*
> 2. *Look at different youth initiatives that are currently taking place in your region or local community. In which areas of youth participation do most of initiatives take place? In your opinion, what is the reason for this?*
> 3. *In which area of youth participation is your organisation/institution involved? Why?*

## 1.2. Benefits of and barriers to youth participation

> *Reflection time*
>
> 1. *What benefits of youth participation would you like to see in your local community or your organisation?*
> 2. *What benefits do you already witness?*

Youth participation can bring very concrete and visible benefits, not only to young people themselves, but also to the organisations/institutions and communities they are involved in. We cannot assume, however, that participation will always bring positive results. Evidence shows that if it is dealt with in an inappropriate way (represented, for example, by the lower rungs of the ladder of participation), it might actually have a negative impact on those involved.[12]

Youth researchers and youth work practitioners indicate that meaningful youth participation:

– *Makes a positive difference in the lives of young people*

Participation should not be seen as an end, a final goal to reach, but as a means to an end or an effective way of achieving a positive change in society. Young people can contribute to this change, especially when they see positive developments in their own lives.

– *Makes young people heard*

Young people, just like other groups in society and the local community, want to have a say about different issues, want to be heard and want to have their views taken seriously. By getting involved they can express their opinions in different fora and have a chance to get their opinions taken into account.

---

11. Thornton, S., *Club cultures: music, media and subcultural capital*, Polity Press, Cambridge, 1995. Quoted after: Griffin, C., "Challenging assumptions about youth political participation: critical insights from Great Britain", Forbrig, J. (ed.), *Revisiting youth political participation. Challenges for research and democratic practice in Europe*, Council of Europe, 2005, p. 152.
12. Kirby, P. and Bryson, S., *Measuring the magic? Evaluating and researching young people's participation in public decision-making*, Carnegie Young People Initiative, London, 2002.

– *Stimulates young people to develop new skills, gain more confidence*

By getting involved in different initiatives young people can acquire new knowledge, develop new skills, attitudes, and leadership ability, and can form their aspirations for the future. This can happen by means of appropriate educational activities, as well as through "learning-by-doing" when fulfilling some concrete tasks. The opportunity to use these new skills and knowledge helps young people to improve their performance, as they can practice them in their immediate environment.

– *Helps adults to recognise young people's talents and potential*

By working with young people and supporting them in achieving new goals, adults get a chance to challenge common stereotypes about youth (that young people lack the required skills or that they are not interested in community life, for example). Adults then often discover that young people are not less gifted, they just need to be given support and the opportunity to demonstrate their talents.

– *Stimulates young people to take responsibility for their own actions and decisions*

Young people learn that the one who takes decisions also carries the responsibility for the consequences (and vice versa – s/he who has responsibility can also take decisions). This means that if young people want to participate at a local level, they need to assume the ownership of their own actions.

– *Helps young people to understand how democracy works and how it should work in real life*

In a democratic system, people should be able to participate in making decisions affecting their lives. These processes can take place in the framework of various institutions or structures and at very different levels, including at local level. Participation at a local level can be a very good starting point for young people to learn more about the workings of a democracy, about its limitations and potential, and to experiment with the rules of democracy in a familiar environment.

– *Creates space for young people to use their talents and strengths for the benefit of the whole community or organisation*

Young people are often highly motivated to use and develop their strengths and talents. It is therefore very important to create opportunities for them to use these talents for the common good, so that the local community can benefit and young people can get satisfaction from their contribution.

– *Helps adults to understand the needs and the point of view of young people*

Working with young people directly and involving them in the consultation process can create an opportunity to get reliable information about young people's needs. Some researchers claim, however, that there is little evidence to prove that consulting young people about their views and needs provides better quality information than other sources (such as consultations with parents or teachers).[13]

– *Develops adults' skills so that they can work efficiently with young people*

When working together with young people, adults have the chance to learn how participatory work in co-operation with youth should function. However, substantial support might be needed (in the form of training courses or literature for individual study, for example) in order that adults can develop the skills necessary to work efficiently with young people.

– *Creates an opportunity for adults to share their knowledge and experience in a non-patronising way*

Young people do not always want to be told what to do. They want to explore and learn by experimenting. They also keep their eyes open and learn by observing those who have more experience and knowledge. If adults do not impose their decisions, young people are more willing to learn from them, and thereby benefit from their experience.

---

13. Ibid., p. 18.

– *Makes the decision-making process more representative*

Young people constitute a relatively large group within local communities. If decisions taken at a local level have an effect on the lives of different groups, all members should have a chance to be heard and to shape the final outcome, in order that their needs can be met. Therefore, if young people participate in a decision-making process, there is a greater chance that their views will be taken into account and their needs met.

– *Stimulates new approaches and ideas in solving local and regional problems*

Traditionally, young people have been involved in decision-making processes only to a limited extent, as adults have exercised power and governance. It has been observed, however, that inviting young people to co-operate in solving the local problems that concern them can bring a new perspective or new and fresh ideas, and can stimulate thinking to go beyond the traditional ways of tackling the problems. Such new ideas and methods are perhaps better suited to the development of contemporary society.

---

***Your task:***

*You are already working on youth participation or you are planning to do so. You understand the importance of identifying positive changes brought into your community or organisation through the involvement of young people. The questions and suggestions below will guide you through the process of planning a change in your local environment.*

*Remark: this exercise is not directly related to planning and implementing a specific project. It is aimed at helping you to introduce such a change.*

1. *When does your project/initiative on youth participation start?*
2. *To what extent will the project evaluation identify the changes that youth involvement has brought in your environment?*
3. *What else (apart from evaluation) needs to or could be done to properly identify the benefits of youth participation in your context?*
4. *Do you feel you have necessary skills and resources (such as time available) to do this work? What are possible ways of developing these skills and obtaining these resources?*
5. *If yes, then:*
   – *decide on which specific areas of the community/organisation operation you want to focus when identifying the benefits of youth participation;*
   – *make a step-by-step plan on how you are going to identify them;*
   – *decide on what kind of support you will need and where you can get it;*
   – *decide on when you want to do this.*
6. *If no, then:*
   – *find out who can do this for you;*
   – *decide together on which specific areas of the community/organisation operation you want to focus when identifying the benefits of youth participation;*
   – *make a step-by-step plan together on how things will be done;*
   – *decide together on what kind of support you will need and where you can get it;*
   – *decide on when the things should be done.*

*Put this into action.*

Those working on youth participation sometimes face challenges and obstacles. Such obstacles might originate from the general situation in a community, the accepted values, political issues, or cultural reasons, etc. Researchers[14] and practitioners mention the following:

- different values and habits of young people and adults;
- different time schedules of young people and adults;
- different communication styles;
- different levels and types of experience;
- lack of skills;
- insufficient support provided to young people and adults;
- lack of expertise on how to involve young people in a meaningful way;
- different learning methods of adults and youth;
- place of youth in the social hierarchy (in some cultures young people traditionally have a very low position and little influence);
- patronising of youth by adults;
- mistrust between adults and young people;
- negative stereotypes ("all young people are …"; "all the adults are …"), mutual misconceptions and biases;
- lack of youth-friendly procedures and policies within organisations (for example, large amounts of formal documents to read, analyse and react to);
- the belief that it is someone else's job to work on youth participation;
- costs related to youth participation;
- location;
- lack of information;
- lack of other necessary resources (extra time, for example);
- high turnover of young people;
- accessibility for disabled people;
- meetings that are too long;
- school commitments;
- other interests;
- belief that nothing will change, even if a young person participates;
- young people who participate are not representative of youth in general.

---

*Reflection time*

1. *What are the biggest barriers to youth participation in your local context?*
2. *What can you do to address these challenges?*
3. *Who can be your ally in this process?*

---

14. See the bibliography at the end of the manual.

Youth participation has not yet been recognised in all communities as being beneficial for their development and coherence. There are different reasons for this, one example being cultural norms that favour hierarchical structures and relationships. In such communities, older people play a very important role and it is considered disrespectful when young people try to get involved in decision-making processes. In such a context it might be not easy to work on youth participation, but the experience of development organisations working in such environments shows that there are efficient ways of dealing with such challenges.[15] They stress the role of community organisations and youth organisations in involving young people in their activities, in initiating a constructive dialogue between the young and older people and in creating tools for efficient co-operation. Another important aim in communities based on hierarchical structures and submission to authority is to work on the attitudes of people who hold positions of power (not only local authority representatives, but also teachers, parents, etc.) so that young people can be perceived as partners.

## 1.3. Principles of youth participation

Earlier in this chapter it was mentioned that there exist different ways of understanding what youth participation is and different ideas about how to support youth involvement. It is maybe a bit less controversial to agree on a set of principles that ensure that youth participation in organisations or communities can be meaningful and effective.

> *Reflection time*
>
> 1. *Try to formulate at least three practices, solutions and recommendations that could strengthen youth participation in the context in which you work.*
> 2. *Do you find it difficult to list such practices? Why?*

To introduce the first three principles of youth participation we can use a model proposed by Marc Jans and Kurt De Backer.[16]

This model indicates that:

– *Participation should be based on a challenge*

"Challenge" here means a theme that should be directly related to the daily reality of young people and which should be engaging or interesting for them;

– *Participation should be based on capacity*

Young people need to have some knowledge and skills in order to get involved. Projects or initiatives should therefore fit the capabilities of the young people concerned and it must be possible for any skills that are lacking to be developed in the framework of the project;

---

15. See, for example, Golombek, S. (ed.), *What works in youth participation: case studies from around the world*, International Youth Foundation, 2002.
16. Jans, M. and De Backer, K., op. cit., p. 5.

– *Participation should be based on connection*

"Young people have to feel connected with and supported by humans, communities, ideas, movements."[17] Essentially, this means that they want to know that they are not alone and that they can identify with and count on a group or institution (to count on them also in the sense of getting the necessary support space).

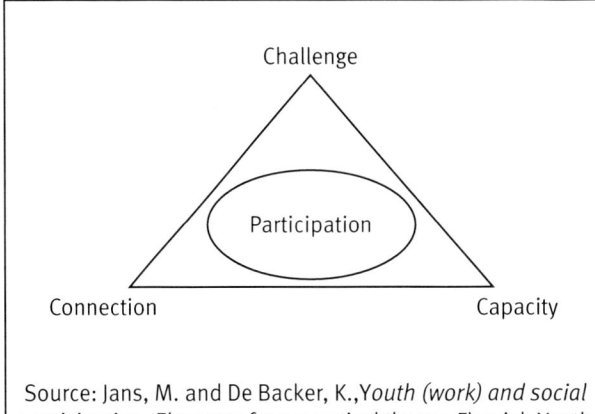

Source: Jans, M. and De Backer, K., *Youth (work) and social participation. Elements for a practical theory*, Flemish Youth Council YeP! 2002, p. 5

Besides the three principles mentioned above, the experience of practitioners working in the field of youth involvement shows that if one wants to achieve meaningful youth participation, then it should be:

– *Available to all young people, regardless of background, nationality, religion, etc.*

The revised charter states that "the principles and various forms of participation advocated in this Charter apply to all young people without discrimination".[18] So access to participation cannot be limited on the basis of such factors such as where somebody comes from or what his/her beliefs are;

– *Voluntary*

This means that participation is not compulsory and young people have the right not to participate if they so choose. They can also decide on the degree and form of their involvement;

– *Related to real needs of young people*

It is important and motivating for young people to get involved in issues that directly affect them; to achieve some positive change, to look for solutions to their problems, to gain new skills or to develop their interests and hobbies. In this way they also feel that they take responsibility for their own lives and communities;

– *Valued*

Everybody should know that his/her contribution is important (even if this contribution is limited);

– *Beneficial to all the actors involved*

Meaningful participation brings benefits to young people, adults, organisations and to communities alike, as it achieves positive changes in different areas – personal development, levels of efficiency, social change, etc.;

---

17. Ibid., p. 6.
18. *The revised European Charter on the Participation of Young People in Local and Regional Life*, Congress of Local and Regional Authorities of the Council of Europe, May 2003.

– *Offer diverse forms of involvement*

One single form of participation appropriate to all young people does not exist. It is therefore important that a variety of ways of getting involved is offered to youth so that they can choose what they find most relevant and interesting;

– *Backed up with the resources needed*

If the resources are not available, access to participation becomes very limited, and for some, impossible. The necessary resources, such as time, human resources, finance, know-how, transportation, etc., need to be provided;

– *Based on real partnership between adults and young people*

Partnership means communicating expectations and fears, negotiating roles, and sharing power and responsibility. It does not always mean sharing all the areas of work and responsibility equally; it means sharing these areas according to what both sides want, need and can contribute;

– *Transparent*

It is necessary that all the parties involved in the process are aware of the purpose of participation and its limits. They should also be clear on what kind of influence young people have, what can be changed and what not;

– *Anchored as a policy principle rather than a mere technique*[19]

"Participation is not one technique or form of involvement. It is complex and it embraces various areas, levels and dimensions. Therefore it should be a transversal element[20] within different policies and strategies planned within organisations or communities";

– *Enjoyable*

In general people (regardless of age) are more likely to undertake actions on a voluntary basis if the work is enjoyable. "Enjoyable" does not necessarily mean fun, but simply something that brings satisfaction or pleasure from accomplishing it.

---

**Reflection time**

1. *Which of the principles of youth participation mentioned above are already present in the work of your organisation/in your community?*
2. *Which principles still need to be implemented and who should be responsible for doing this?*
3. *How can you contribute to introducing these new principles?*

---

19. Forbrig, J., op. cit. p. 16.
20. Transversal means that it concerns different aspects and areas of life.

## 1.4. Preconditions for youth participation

Participation does not just happen; it does not develop out of nothing. A number of conditions must be fulfilled so that meaningful participation can be practised. These so-called preconditions to youth participation can be simply explained as practices or values that have to exist, or need to be developed, in a community or organisation interested in strengthening youth involvement. There is no fixed set of preconditions that could be used as a checklist for those who are trying to achieve meaningful participation; they need to be defined for each specific context by the actors who operate within it and who know this context very well.

Some examples of conditions encouraging youth participation:

- the ability to deal constructively with a conflict situation;
- access to participation for those who are not members of any structures;
- access to information;
- access to technology;
- an active youth sector;
- awareness of the value of participation;
- basic needs should be fulfilled (food, drink, clothing, habitat, etc.);
- equality (opinions of adults and young people have equal weight);
- an existing youth-adult partnership;
- financial resources;
- having a choice of the most appropriate or interesting area or form of involvement;
- having the local needs identified;
- involvement of different actors;
- knowledge about young people's situation, identity, lifestyle, etc., in a community;
- legal framework;
- minimum level of education;
- openness to learn, also from one's mistakes;
- participation infrastructure;
- participation-friendly policies;
- physical and emotional security;
- representation of the interests of disadvantaged youth;
- right to participate;
- skills and competencies in management and participatory processes;
- an understanding of what meaningful participation is (as opposed to tokenism);
- willingness to participate or to undertake participatory work;
- willingness to share power and control.

For meaningful youth participation, all of the above-mentioned preconditions have to be fulfilled, otherwise the quality of participation will not be as high as it could be in a specific setting. That is why, when aiming at an efficient level of involvement of young people in an organisation or community, it is necessary to check to what extent these preconditions are fulfilled and what deficits still need to be addressed.

> ***Your task:***
> 1. *Go back to the list of preconditions to youth participation.*
> 2. *Identify the preconditions that are already fulfilled in your organisation, community or project.*
> 3. *Describe in what way or to what extent they have been already met.*
> 4. *Decide which of them needs to be implemented even further.*
> 5. *Brainstorm on how this can be achieved and by whom.*

> 6. *Identify the preconditions that have not yet been met in your organisation, community or project.*
> 7. *Try to think of possible reasons why these preconditions have not yet been fulfilled.*
> 8. *Brainstorm how they can be achieved and by whom.*
> 9. *Make a realistic plan of action for yourself, in which you plan how you personally will contribute to the implementation of the preconditions needed for meaningful youth participation.*

## 1.5. Forms of youth participation

There are many ways in which young people can participate in taking decisions about issues important to them and to the whole local community. Some forms of participation seem to be more appealing to young people than others; some can be more relevant in a specific context than others and each has some potential as well as its limitations.

The most common forms of youth participation observed in contemporary European societies are as follows:

- voluntary work;
- participating in different forms of non-formal education;
- peer education – involvement of young people in educating their peers (for example, health promotion programmes, awareness-raising campaigns, etc.);
- being active in an organisation/club and taking responsibility for some areas of its work;
- youth councils, parliaments, fora, boards and other structures – a traditional way of participating in decision-making processes in the framework of international, national, regional or local authorities, schools, clubs, NGOs, etc.;
- co-management systems existing in some institutions (for example, in the Directorate of Youth and Sport of the Council of Europe) where the decisions are taken by representatives of young people or youth organisations and representatives of the authorities on an equal basis;
- consultations – used in decision-making processes to voice needs and concerns and to make proposals;
- different levels of participation of young people in projects and activities (organised as well as non-organised);
- campaigning activities;
- membership of political parties, unions, interest groups;
- taking part in elections (both to vote and to be elected).

When looking at how many young people are actually involved in the above-mentioned forms of participation, it becomes clear that the numbers are steadily decreasing. This does not mean, however, that young people are losing interest in participation. It turns out that "most show a clear will to participate and to influence the choices made by society, but they wish to do so on a more individual and more one-off basis, outside of the old participatory structures and mechanisms".[21] This conclusion has very important consequences for practitioners

---
21. EU White Paper, "A new impetus for European youth", COM (2001) 681 final, p. 10.

working on youth participation – young people should have the chance to experiment and to find the right ways of getting involved, even if this means focusing on the non-traditional forms of participation. There is currently no clear definition of what "new forms of participation" means exactly, but different sources mention the following examples:

- peer-to-peer networks;
- discussion fora;
- signing petitions;
- participation in so-called "new social movements";
- support groups;
- boycotting of products;
- demonstrations;
- international meetings;
- using the Internet to gather information, express views or influence decision-making processes.

Individuals, organisations and communities promoting youth participation and looking for new ways of involving young people need to be very clear what their motivations are. Do they want to reach a higher number of young people so that the official statistics look better? Or do they perhaps want to find the best and most meaningful ways for youth to become involved and to contribute? Or maybe there are some other reasons? It seems that attention should not be focused only on getting as many young people as possible to participate, but also on ways of ensuring a better quality of participation.

> *Reflection time*
>
> 1. Which forms of youth participation are the most common in your community or organisation?
> 2. Why do you think this is?
> 3. Do you think that creating the right conditions for other forms of youth participation in your context would encourage more efficient participation of young people? Why?
> 4. To what extent can, in your opinion, non-participation of young people be considered as a form of participation? Why do you think some young people do not participate and what do they want to achieve by that?
> 5. Can you think of other forms of participation than those mentioned above?

# Chapter 2

## The revised European Charter on the Participation of Young People in Local and Regional Life

### 2.1. Introduction

*What is the revised European Charter on the Participation of Young People in Local and Regional Life?*

Youth participation has a high priority in the work of the Council of Europe, especially in the Directorate of Youth and Sport and the Congress of Local and Regional Authorities of the Council of Europe. Numerous initiatives have been undertaken to promote youth involvement and to equip those needing them with the necessary tools and skills. Examples of these are a co-management system,[22] training events and other educational activities, research activities and financial support to youth projects promoting participation.[23]

A very specific tool used to promote youth participation at the local and regional level is the revised European Charter on the Participation of Young People in Local and Regional Life; a document adopted by the Congress of Local and Regional Authorities of the Council of Europe in May 2003. The charter presents concrete ideas and instruments that can be used in a local context by those involved in participation work – young people, youth organisations, local authorities, etc. It does not, however, offer a ready-to-use template, due to the fact that needs and circumstances differ widely throughout Europe. Thus the charter should be seen as a source of recommendations and inspiration, rather than a strict recipe for the promotion of youth participation at local and regional levels.

---

22. Through a unique partnership between the representatives of youth organisations and governments, the Council of Europe created a system of co-management within the Directorate of Youth and Sport, which gives young people the opportunity to have their say in the formulation and implementation of the Council of Europe's youth policy. More information about co-management can be found in Chapter 7 of this manual.

23. Every year the European Youth Foundation provides financial support to numerous projects promoting youth participation at local, national and international level in Europe.

### *What is the Congress of Local and Regional Authorities of the Council of Europe?*

The revised European Charter on the Participation of Young People in Local and Regional Life was initiated and adopted by the Congress of Local and Regional Authorities of the Council of Europe, one of the political institutions of the Organisation. The Congress gives advice to the Committee of Ministers regarding various aspects of local and regional policy. It brings together elected representatives of both local and regional authorities from the Council of Europe's member states.

The Congress' main role is to promote democracy at local and regional level, because democracy begins in the towns and villages of Europe. As Halvdan Skard, President of the Congress, said: "The Congress has become one of the main bodies safeguarding local and regional democracy throughout Europe and a key political partner in dialogue with governments."

The activities of the Congress focus on:

– supporting the introduction and the development of self-government at local and regional levels;

– enhancing constructive dialogue between local and regional authorities and national authorities;

– monitoring local democracy in European regions and municipalities;

– monitoring local and regional elections;

The Congress consists of two chambers: the Chamber of Local Authorities and the Chamber of Regions. The 318 members and the 318 substitutes of both chambers represent 200 000 European municipalities and regions and are appointed by their national associations of local and regional authorities.

Four statutory committees, dealing with different issues, elaborate reports and political texts for the chambers. One of these is the Culture and Education Committee, which is responsible for youth issues.

The Congress actively seeks to ensure the widest possible dissemination of the revised charter. Although the revised charter was drawn up by the Congress the responsibility of the implementation of this document lies with the local and regional authorities.

---

*Your task:*

1. Find out who are the delegates of your country to the Chamber of Local Authorities and the Chamber of Regions (the list is available on the Congress website).

2. Contact them and ask for more information on what has been done in your country to promote and implement the revised charter, and what further actions are planned.

3. Ask how you can contribute to the promotion and implementation of the charter.

4. Think of possible ways of becoming involved and of encouraging the involvement of your organisation, local community or local authorities.

---

### *How and why was the charter revised?*

The European Charter on the Participation of Young People in Municipal and Regional Life (the original name of the document) was adopted in March 1992 by the Standing Conference of Local and Regional Authorities of the Council of Europe (renamed in 1994 as "the Congress of Local and Regional Authorities in Europe"). In spite of its potential, the document was neither widely known, nor sufficiently used by the Council of Europe member states.[24] Ten years later, the Congress and the Directorate of Youth and Sport organised the Conference "Young People – Actors in their Towns and Regions" in Cracow (7-8 March 2002) to celebrate the 10th anniversary of the European charter and to evaluate the successes and challenges for youth participation during the first decade of the charter's existence.[25] The conference also focused on further promotion of youth participation and good practices in this field.

In its final declaration, the conference formulated a request for amendment of the European charter, as it was concluded that the provisions of the charter did not sufficiently reflect new developments in contemporary society.

> *Reflection time*
>
> 1. What are the new social, political, economic or technological developments that have an impact on the lives, needs and aspirations of young people?
> 2. Which of these developments can have a major influence on young people's participation (both globally and in your community or organisation)?

As a result of the request, an expert group was formed consisting of representatives of the Congress and the Advisory Council on Youth of the Council of Europe,[26] and other experts, and work began on the revision of the charter. The revised European Charter on the Participation of Young People in Local and Regional Life was adopted by the Congress in May 2003 (as Appendix to Recommendation 128).

The revised charter addresses new developments affecting the lives of young people in contemporary European society, such as the growing influence of the Internet among young people, youth unemployment, or the consequences of urban insecurity. Moreover, it contains a review of local policies dealing with issues that are important to young people, and proposes ways in which these policies can support youth participation at a local level.

### *The revised charter in different languages*

The charter has been published in the two official languages of the Council of Europe – English and French – but translations into several other European languages also exist.[27] The process of translating the charter into all the official languages of the Council of Europe's member states is still ongoing, so that in future it will be accessible by local communities throughout Europe.

---

24. Doorley, J., "Synthesis report on the work of the Council of Europe's Directorate of Youth and Sport in the field of youth participation and democratic citizenship between 2003 and 2005 and an analysis of current trends in youth participation and recommendations for future action", CDEJ (2006)4, Strasbourg, January 2006, p. 6.

25. Introduction to the revised European Charter on the Participation of Young People in Local and Regional Life, Congress of Local and Regional Authorities of the Council of Europe, May 2003, p. 5.

26. The Advisory Council on Youth is a statutory body of the Council of Europe, composed of 30 representatives of non-governmental youth organisations and networks. Its main role is to formulate recommendations on policy and programme issues in the youth sector of the Council of Europe.

27. The existing translations can be found on the Congress website at: www.coe.int/t/congress or on the website of the European Knowledge Centre for Youth Policy at: www.training-youth.net and www.youth-knowledge.net/INTEGRATION/EKC/GP/charter.html.

The revised charter is an official document of the Council of Europe and is therefore written in a formal style that might seem rather difficult to understand for those not used to working with legal documents, and particularly for young people. That is why a so-called "plain language" version of the revised charter has been created, in which the principles and recommendations are illustrated through examples and explained in simple, "youth-friendly" language. This plain language version is available on an interactive CD-Rom and online,[28] so that young people can become familiar with the charter in a less formal way.

> *Your task:*
>
> 1. Find out if the revised charter has been already translated into your language (both the official and the plain language versions).
> 2. If not, do you know an organisation, institution or a group that would be willing to translate the charter into your language? Would you be willing to get involved in organising the translation?
> 3. Contact possible partners and plan the translation process.
> 4. Implement your plan.
> 5. Send the translated version to the Directorate of Youth and Sport of the Council of Europe (youth@coe.int) and to the Secretariat of the Congress (congress.web@coe.int) so that it can be made accessible to other people too.
> 6. If a translation exists, find out:
>    – where printed copies of the charter can be obtained in your country;
>    – if the charter's translation is accessible online. If so, on which websites?
> 7. Order as many copies of the charter as you will need.
> 8. Find out whether the plain language version of the charter exists in your language and whether you can have access to it.

### Legal status of the charter

Recommendation Rec(2004)13 of the Committee of Ministers supporting the implementation of the revised charter has been adopted by all member states of the Council of Europe.[29] In practice, this means that member states have a moral responsibility to implement the revised charter, although its recommendations are not legally binding. The charter should therefore be seen as a set of principles, best practices and guidelines to enhance youth participation at local and regional levels.

---

28. Available at: www.youth-knowledge.net/INTEGRATION/EKC/GP/charter.html.
29. At the time of printing (autumn 2007) the Council of Europe has 47 member states: Albania, Andorra, Armenia, Austria, Azerbaijan, Belgium, Bosnia and Herzegovina, Bulgaria, Croatia, Cyprus, Czech Republic, Denmark, Estonia, Finland, France, Georgia, Germany, Greece, Hungary, Iceland, Ireland, Italy, Latvia, Liechtenstein, Lithuania, Luxembourg, Malta, Moldova, Monaco, Montenegro, Netherlands, Norway, Poland, Portugal, Romania, Russian Federation, San Marino, Serbia, Slovakia, Slovenia, Spain, Sweden, Switzerland, "the former Yugoslav Republic of Macedonia", Turkey, Ukraine, United Kingdom. The updated list can be found at: www.coe.int/T/e/com/about_coe/member_states/default.asp.

## 2.2. Content of the charter

The charter consists of three parts relating to different aspects of youth participation at a local level.

### Part I – Sectoral policies

Active participation by young people depends on a number of internal factors, such as motivation, needs and aspirations, and external factors, such as situation, infrastructure and existing systems. Local policies play a very powerful role in creating the right conditions and infrastructure for young people to participate in the life of their schools, organisations or communities and so the revised charter contains a review of different policy areas and suggests a number of concrete measures that can provide the necessary support for youth involvement. These suggestions, however, remain rather general, so that communities throughout Europe can find the most appropriate ways of putting these measures into practice, taking into account their own local context and background.

| Policy area | Recommendations for the local and regional authorities |
|---|---|
| Policy for sport, leisure and associative life | – to support activities run by youth associations and organisations, youth groups and local centres; <br> – to support organisations training local youth workers, facilitators and leaders of youth clubs and organisations; <br> – to encourage associations to promote youth participation in their statutory bodies. |
| Policy to promote youth employment and to combat unemployment | – to develop policies and programmes to combat youth unemployment and to promote employment opportunities for young people; <br> – to establish local employment centres; <br> – to support the setting up of business activities by young people; <br> – to encourage experimentation with social economy, self-help initiatives or co-operatives. |
| Urban environment and habitat, housing policy and transport | – to create conditions for developing an urban environment policy based on a more integrated, less fragmented living environment; <br> – to pursue housing and urban environment policies; <br> – to draw up programmes for a more harmonious environment; <br> – to develop local information services on housing; <br> – to develop local schemes to help young people to gain access to housing; <br> – to involve young people in the organisation of public transport; <br> – to support rural transport initiatives that seek to provide transport services. |

| | |
|---|---|
| An education and training policy promoting youth participation | – to actively encourage the participation of young people in school life;<br>– to provide financial and other support (for example, meeting facilities) to enable young people to establish democratic school student associations;<br>– to ensure that students and student associations are consulted regularly concerning curricula and other developments. |
| A policy for mobility and exchanges | – to support groups and associations that favour the mobility of young people;<br>– to encourage young people, schools and organisations to take part in international exchanges and networks;<br>– to include youth representatives in twinning committees or other organs co-ordinating such exchanges. |
| A health policy | – to create or develop institutional mechanisms for consultations between young people, organisations and other groups concerned with social welfare and health promotion;<br>– to introduce, develop or promote local information policies and counselling facilities for young people affected by tobacco, alcohol or drug abuse;<br>– to develop special training policies for social and youth workers and leaders involved in prevention and rehabilitation work;<br>– to intensify information campaigns and preventive measures related to sexually transmitted diseases. |
| A gender equality policy | – to support young men and women in obtaining positions of responsibility within professional life, associations, politics, local and regional authorities;<br>– to promote an educational policy of equality between men and women by drawing up a plan aiming at eliminating inequalities and by implementing and evaluating measures promoting equal opportunities;<br>– to enable girls and young women to receive information on training courses;<br>– to offer grants and specific courses to girls and young women;<br>– to introduce quotas of places reserved for women in institutions dealing with public affairs<br>– to introduce financial measures for social services. |
| A specific policy for rural areas | – to ensure that different sectoral policies reflect and address the special needs of young people living in rural areas;<br>– to provide support to youth organisations and community organisations active in rural areas. |

| A policy on access to culture | – to adopt policies allowing young people to become cultural actors;<br>– to adopt policies which will facilitate access to knowledge, the practice of culture and to creative activity. |
|---|---|
| A policy to combat violence and crime | – to include young people in crime prevention councils;<br>– to work with young people at risk of being involved in or already involved in crime;<br>– to combat racist violence;<br>– to tackle violence in schools;<br>– to contribute to the creation of networks or projects promoting non-violence and tolerance;<br>– to protect young people from sexual exploitation and abuse;<br>– to create structures providing support to victims of sexual exploitation and abuse. |
| An anti-discrimination policy | – to actively promote human rights;<br>– to reinforce anti-discrimination legislation;<br>– to ensure equal access for all citizens to public places, vocational training, schooling, housing and to cultural activities, etc.;<br>– to include inter-religious dialogue, multicultural, anti-racist and anti-discrimination education as a part of school curriculum. |
| A policy on sexuality | – to promote non-directive sex education in schools;<br>– to support organisations and services offering information about relationships and sexuality;<br>– to support peer work in this field. |
| A policy of access to rights and law | – to disseminate information about the rights of young people;<br>– to support services designed to work on the application of young people's rights;<br>– to allow young people to participate in the drawing-up of new rules. |

## Part II – Instruments for youth participation

The next part of the charter focuses on ideas and tools that can be used by local authorities to enhance youth participation. They relate to concrete areas in which youth participation can be implemented in a meaningful way.

Area 1: Training in youth participation
- vocational training for teachers and youth workers in the practice of youth participation
- implementing all forms of participation of pupils in schools;
- introducing civic education programmes in schools (training in youth participation, human rights, etc.);
- introducing peer-group education, providing the necessary resources and supporting the exchange of good practice.

Area 2: Informing young people
- supporting or creating youth information centres or counselling centres;
- taking specific measures to meet the needs of young people who have problems with accessing information (the disabled, those with no Internet access or no knowledge of computers, those living in disadvantaged neighbourhoods or rural areas, etc.);
- creating and guaranteeing standards regarding information services for young people;
- ensuring that information services conform to these standards.

Area 3: Promoting youth participation through information and communication technologies
- using information and communication technologies as part of the information and participation policies of local authorities;
- guaranteeing young people access to these technologies (both infrastructure and know-how).

Area 4: Promoting youth participation in media
- supporting the creation and operation of local media developed by and for young people;
- ensuring relevant training programmes for young people on how to organise these media.

Area 5: Encouraging young people to undertake voluntary work
- supporting the establishment of volunteer centres;
- providing information on opportunities for voluntary work;
- developing systems which recognise and validate voluntary activity.

Area 6: Supporting young people's projects and initiatives
- facilitating the implementation of young people's projects;
- providing professional help to run these projects;
- providing financial, material and technical assistance.

Area 7: Promoting young people's organisations
- ensuring a specific budget to support youth organisations (with preference given to organisations run by and for young people);
- implementing the co-management principle and system of decision-making in partnership with young people and youth organisations in relevant areas.

Area 8: Promoting youth participation in non-governmental organisations and political parties
- providing resources (also financial) to non-governmental organisations promoting the participation of young people;
- promoting the involvement of young people in the political party system.

*Part III – Institutional participation by young people in local and regional affairs*

The last part of the revised charter contains recommendations with regard to involvement of young people in local structures or institutions. If the sectoral policies (reviewed in Part I) are to be implemented in such a way that they support youth participation at the level of the whole community, the appropriate structures representing views of young people in this respect need to be established. The charter underlines the fact that the final form of institutional participation should be chosen according to local needs, but it should always aim at creating a partnership between youth and local authorities and give an opportunity to young people to become involved in the decisions affecting them.

Recommendations regarding youth councils, youth parliaments, youth forums

- they should be permanent structures;
- they should be composed of elected or appointed representatives from youth organisations;
- their membership should reflect the sociological make-up of the community;
- young people should have direct responsibility for projects and influencing policies;
- they should constitute a physical framework for young people to express their views and concerns (also in relation to initiatives of local authorities);
- they should have the power to make proposals to local authorities;
- they should facilitate consultations with young people and their organisations on issues that concern them;
- they should be a forum to develop, monitor and evaluate young people's projects;
- they should facilitate the participation of young people in other consultative bodies at local level.

Recommendations related to support for structures of youth participation

- local authorities should provide both formal and informal structures for youth participation through the provision of necessary space, financial and material support (although they are also responsible for looking for additional support from other sources);
- local authorities should provide a guarantor who would be responsible for monitoring implementation of the support structures;
- the guarantor should be independent and his nomination agreed between youth representatives and local authorities;
- the guarantor should act as an intermediary between young people and elected local representatives, should represent the interests of young people in cases of misunderstanding or conflict between youth and local authorities and should be a channel of communication between the two.

## 2.3. Target groups of the charter

The revised charter is a document addressed to all those people that are responsible for, involved in or interested in enhancing youth participation in a local context. Each person will probably look at the charter from a different perspective and will want to use it in his or her own way, but the ultimate goal for everybody will be the same: to ensure that young people have the right, means, space, opportunities and support in order to participate and to engage meaningfully in the initiatives and decision-making processes affecting their lives. These five keywords – right, means, space, opportunities and support are the main elements of the charter's approach to participation and they will be explained more in detail in Chapter 3 of this manual.

Main target groups to whom the charter is addressed:

- *Young people*

    Young people comprise a significant part of the population. They are a diverse group, a group having its own needs and aspirations that can be better fulfilled if young people have a say and can play a meaningful role in addressing issues important to them.

- *Informal groups of young people*

    Some young people enjoy sharing their ideas and mixing with other young people, but they do not want to become either official members of associations or part of any structured entity. They might instead choose informal groups that are not registered, that have very flexible rules and meet their needs more efficiently than would hierarchical or organised associations. Such informal groups can exist in the form of spontaneous networks, support groups or as virtual communities, to give a few examples.

- *Young people's organisations and associations*

    Being a member of a youth organisation, youth council or board is one of the traditional forms of youth participation. Ideally, young people should be in leadership positions, but some youth organisations are run either by adults alone or by a partnership between youth and adults. Young people's organisations or associations are usually registered by local or national authorities and can act as legal entities. As such, the presence of adults in leadership positions is required in some countries, where young people might not be held legally responsible for the acts of the organisation.

- *Educational institutions*

    Schools are one of the key places where young people learn new things about the world, form their opinions and get ready for next phase in their lives. Most young people spend a big part of their lives at school or university and so these are places where youth participation should be not only promoted, but also practised.

- *Other organisations*

    There are a number of other organisations working in the field of youth participation that do not work directly with young people or whose membership is open to a variety of different professional groups or age ranges. Such organisations run, for example, educational activities for youth workers or teachers, focus on research, or lobby for reinforcing youth friendly policies.

- *Local authorities*

    There is a growing practice within European countries to create special units within local authorities to deal with young people's concerns. Whether it is a single person or a whole department working in this field, their aim should be to encourage youth participation in a local context, and to support different youth activities and initiatives. However, it is not enough if only representatives directly responsible for youth are using the revised charter. As already mentioned, young people are affected by a number of different sectoral policies and therefore other units within the structure of local authorities should also be involved in the charter's implementation.

When looking at the charter one gets the impression that the document is addressed mainly to local authorities, as it focuses to a large extent on local policies and instruments. Indeed, the authorities have a very important role in creating the right conditions for youth participation at a local level, but they cannot and should not do so without the co-operation and support of young people and their organisations. That is why all the above-mentioned target groups need to get involved, albeit in different capacities or roles, to ensure that the principles and recommendations of the charter can be successfully implemented in a specific community. In the next chapters of the manual, more details will be given about how each of the groups can get involved in the implementation of the charter at a local level.

# CHAPTER 3
## The Charter's approach to participation

### 3.1. Introduction to the charter's approach to youth participation

The revised charter is addressed to various groups involved in promoting youth participation at a local level. Although a substantial part of the document contains recommendations for different sectoral policies, it goes much further than the policy aspects of youth participation. It proposes an approach that can be used in all areas of young people's involvement at local level, such as when running participatory projects for youth, building youth-adult partnerships or setting up youth organisations and groups, etc.

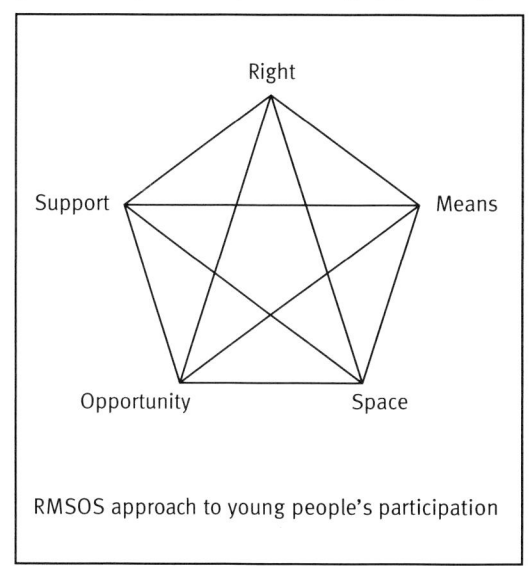

RMSOS approach to young people's participation

The charter's approach to participation is the so-called "RMSOS" approach and is based on the five keywords mentioned in the document's preamble: right, means, space, opportunity and support.[30] It is based on the principle that meaningful youth participation can only take place when the right conditions have been created and all the actors involved in participatory work have been given the responsibility to ensure that these conditions are present.

The five keywords, Right, Means, Space, Opportunity and Support, represent the main factors having an influence on youth involvement at local level (they will be explained more in detail later in this chapter). Each of them focuses on a different support measure, but they are closely interrelated, and they all have to be fulfilled for young people to be able to participate fully in the activities or decisions that interest them.

---

30. These keywords were mentioned in the preamble to the charter and they relate to the understanding of participation that has been embraced in the document: "Participation and active citizenship is about having the right, the means, the space and the opportunity and where necessary the support to participate in and influence decisions and engage in actions and activities so as to contribute to building a better society."

The RMSOS approach can be a useful tool for young people, youth workers or local authorities as it helps them to look critically at their projects or initiatives and to find out whether the right conditions for young people's participation have been created. A more detailed description of the framework provided by the RMSOS approach[31] can be found below.

## 3.2. RMSOS framework

The RMSOS framework is a means of assessing the extent to which each of the five main factors influencing youth participation is present within a project, initiative, organisation or in community life.

### *Right*

Young people have an implicit right to participate and, as has been already mentioned in Chapter 1, it is referred to as a human right or citizen's right. Ideally, there should be a law at local and/or regional level stating that young people have to be consulted and have the right to participate in issues, actions and decisions affecting them. But even in communities where no such law officially exists, young people have a right to participate. In other words, it is not dependent on local or regional authorities to grant such a right, but it is a fundamental right that all young people have and should demand.

Young people should be active in promoting their rights. In practice, this means much more than influencing local decisions by consultations or voting. It implies that the activities, projects or organisations should promote rights that young people have in all areas of life, and this means not only civil or political rights, but also social, economic or cultural ones.

---

*Reflection time*

Rights in general

1. What rights do young people have?
2. What rights does your project/organisation seek to address or promote?
3. How do you know that these rights are relevant to the young people addressed by your project?

Right to participate

1. Do young people have a right to participate in your local community? How do you know this?
2. Do they have the rights necessary to practice participation (for example, the right to express their opinion, the right to be heard, etc.)? What are these rights specifically?
3. How does your project seek to promote or address the right of young people to participate in issues, actions and decisions that have an influence on their lives?

---

31. The description of the framework has been adapted from materials prepared for the training course on the development and implementation of participatory projects at local and regional level, which took place in June 2005 at the European Youth Centre in Strasbourg.

Rights of young people within your project, organisation or community

1. What role do young people play in the decision making within your project, organisation or community?
2. Are they present at all levels of decision making?
3. Do they have the necessary autonomy and responsibility to make decisions and to implement them within your project?
4. How do the young people involved in your project develop the skills needed for effective decision making?
5. How and to what extent is your project open to all young people, without discrimination on the basis of their national, ethnic, religious and cultural identities, social class, economic resources, gender, sexual orientation, physical ability, etc?

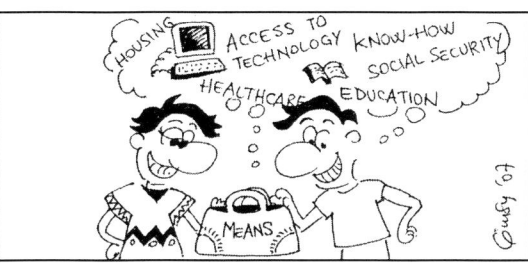

## Means

Life can be more difficult for young people who have insufficient resources in life (financial resources, for example) and who live in poverty due to unemployment or other difficulties. This may mean that their basic needs like food or shelter are not met and they may feel isolated or left out of society as a result. It is natural that, in such circumstances, the priority is to try to look for different ways of obtaining the missing resources and, as a result, young people might lack the time or motivation to participate in the life of an organisation or community.

In order to encourage young people to get involved, therefore, it has to be ensured that basic needs are met. These include sufficient social security, education, housing, health care, transportation, know-how and access to technology.

### Reflection time

1. What are the most important means that young people need in your local context so that they can fully participate in your project, organisation or community life? How have you identified these needs?
2. What issues relating to these means does your project or organisation address (if any)? In what way?
3. How are issues such as means/resources, access, location or distance dealt with by your project, organisation or community?
4. How do these affect the possibilities for the young people you are addressing to get involved in your project?
5. What practical and relevant resources do you have or need for a diverse range of young people to be able to get involved in your project (transport, expenses or interpreters, for example)? How can you obtain the resources that you do not yet have?
6. Is your project or organisation accessible for young people with disabilities or who are disadvantaged? What support is necessary to help them get involved and how is it provided?

*Space*

Young people need physical space to meet, to spend time or to organise their own activities. As far as participation in school activities or other organised curricula is concerned, facilities are usually provided (in classrooms, gyms or youth clubs, for example). But it is much more difficult for young people to find a place to meet in if they are interested in getting involved in non-organised initiatives. That is why we are seeing the Internet being used more and more frequently by young people as a space for exchanging views or even setting up projects with other like-minded people.

But this RMSOS factor is not only about physical space, it is much more about the space to participate within the institutional framework of policy making. This essentially means that young people's views, recommendations and conclusions should have a real impact on decisions that are made. Very often young people are invited to participate in processes, but in fact they have little possibility to influence and shape the final outcome. This is called "token representation".

---

*Reflection time*

1. *What space is available for young people in your community (physical, virtual, institutional)? Is it, in your opinion, sufficient?*
2. *In what ways can young people have a real impact on the final outcome of the decisions that influence their lives?*
3. *To what extent does your project or organisation help young people to have a bigger influence on the final outcome of the decisions affecting their lives?*
4. *How does your project or organisation empower young people involved in the project to express their views, opinions, desires and concerns about the way the community/local environment or the project develops?*
5. *What practical measures can you apply in your context to make sure that young people's views have a real impact?*
6. *Question for project organisers: is the space in which the project will take place accessible, welcoming and open to all? Who has designed the space and on the basis of what criteria?*

*Opportunity*

In order to be able to participate actively young people need to be provided with the opportunity to do so. This means, for example, that young people must have easy access to information on how to get involved, what the opportunities available are and where they are. When they know what is going on in their local community in terms of youth participation they can make informed decisions about their involvement. It is sometimes the case that young people do not participate, not because they have no interest, but simply because they do not get information about existing opportunities.

Secondly, events, decision-making processes and systems need to be youth-friendly. There should not only be space for young people within these processes and structures, but the way they are organised and the way they work should be such that young people can understand them and can fully contribute if they so wish. It therefore has to be ensured, for example, that young people have the opportunity to participate in terms of having sufficient time and supportive structures.

> *Reflection time*
>
> 1. *What are the opportunities for youth participation in your local context or your organisation?*
> 2. *How are these opportunities communicated to young people? Is it efficient?*
> 3. *How will your project influence the opportunity of young people to participate at a local and/or regional level?*
> 4. *How can young people get involved in your project? How do they find out about it? Is it youth friendly?*
> 5. *In what way(s) does your project give young people the opportunity to practice democracy and citizenship?*
> 6. *In what way(s) does your project give educational opportunities to young people?*
> 7. *What kind of young people can participate in your project? Do these young people already hold leadership positions?*

## Support

Young people have lots of talent and the potential to participate, but without the necessary support, their involvement might not be as efficient as it could be. They should have access to various forms of support. These include, for example, financial, moral and institutional support at a number of different levels – personal, organisational or at local community level. Ideally, local authorities should provide adequate financial support to cover expenses and structural costs, but it is still the case that in many communities, youth issues do not have priority in terms of local financial management.

Young people also need to have access to moral support and advice. This can be provided, for example, by a person referred to in the revised charter as a guarantor[32] or, alternatively, by a youth worker or other professional who has the necessary experience and expertise in working in the field of youth-adult partnerships or in working with young people. Lastly, the institution or community as a whole needs to support and recognise the importance and contribution of youth participation, not only for young people, but also for public authorities and society in general.

### Reflection time

1. In what way is your local community environment supportive of the participation of young people?
2. Can your project or organisation improve the situation? How?
3. Is the participation of youth a part of the culture of your community or organisation? How can you prove this?
4. In what way are the structures and policies in your organisation or community youth-friendly?
5. What kind of institutional support do you have for your project? What does this mean in practice? How does it support participation of young people in the project?
6. Is the assistance of adults limited to the indirect management of your project ("backing up youth leadership") or are adults the project managers? What are the consequences of this (both advantages and limitations) for your project?
7. What skills do young people need to actively participate in your project?
8. Do you have competent support staff (voluntary or professional) in your organisation to support the involvement of young people in your project? If so, what skills do they have?

---

32. The charter explains that a guarantor is an independent person or a group of persons who will make sure that the necessary support for the participation of young people is provided, who will act as an intermediary between young people and local authorities and, if necessary, will represent young people in cases of conflict. See: the revised charter, point III.2.68-70.

It has been already mentioned that all five elements of the RMSOS approach need to be present in order that meaningful participation by young people can take place. If, for example, their right to participate is denied, it does not matter what means, space or support will be provided, they will not be able to get involved. On the other hand, having the right, but insufficient support means that this right cannot be exercised. Although each of the RMSOS factors has been analysed separately in this chapter, one therefore needs to see all the elements as parts of an interconnected system, one that is balanced and operates well only when all the elements function properly.

# CHAPTER 4
## The Charter in practice

### 4.1. The revised charter as a practical tool for different actors

Chapter 1 of this manual discussed the different reasons and motivations behind the participation of young people and concluded that it is impossible to create one approach that would meet the needs of all and that would be suitable for all situations and contexts.

The revised charter outlines the policies and principles necessary for meaningful youth participation and it deals with a wide range of issues affecting the lives of young people at local and regional level in Europe. As a Council of Europe document, the charter aims at addressing very diverse situations (both geographic, economic, social, political and cultural) throughout Europe and it provides a framework that can be tailored to the specific needs and circumstances of various communities and organisations, rather than a detailed, ready-to-use prescription. It should therefore not be seen as a static document, but rather as a dynamic set of suggestions that can be used in the most relevant way in a given context.

The three parts of the charter contain guidelines for different groups interested in youth participation on how to create the right conditions for the involvement of young people. Such groups might use the charter in the ways that are most relevant for them and might try to achieve a wide range of aims. In practice, this means that they will focus on different areas addressed by the charter and not necessarily on the whole document at the same time.

> *Reflection time*
> 1. *Who are the potential groups/actors in your own context that could be interested in using the charter as a tool to promote youth participation?*
> 2. *Why would they be interested in using the charter?*
> 3. *What are your links (if any) with any such groups or institutions?*
> 4. *Are they aware that the charter exists? How do you know?*

Very different groups or actors operating within a local context can use the recommendations proposed in the charter in their own individual ways. In this manual, however, the focus will be put on three main groups responsible for promoting youth participation at the local and regional levels, namely young people, youth organisations and local authorities.

### *Young people*

Young people comprise a significant part of the population in many local communities, yet their role and influence is rather limited when it comes to dealing with local issues. The charter offers a number of concrete ideas on how to strengthen the role of young people in local decision-making processes and, for this reason, it is an important tool for young people to create better conditions for their meaningful involvement in public life. The charter contains a number of recommendations that should be followed by local authorities and young people can therefore use it as a unique tool to lobby their local authorities to promote youth participation. Young people can also play an active role in disseminating the charter in their local context among different institutions, at schools and in clubs, etc. The potential of the charter can be used only if the relevant actors are aware of its existence and if they know how to make the best of it for their local community.

Young people need to be empowered in order to use the charter and to follow its recommendations. Although they might have the potential and motivation, there are a number of skills and attitudes that need to be developed, and some extra knowledge that needs to be gained. Without empowerment it might be very difficult, if not impossible, for young people in some circumstances to get involved and to contribute to the lives of their communities.

### *Organisations*

When talking about organisations, one should keep in mind that these do not have to be registered or officially existing associations, but can also be non-formalised groups, ad hoc networks, etc. Some organisations working on promoting youth participation do allow young people to become members, but a number of them restrict membership to adults only.[33] All of them, however, can play a vital role in creating opportunities and the right environment for young people to become involved and they can use the charter in a variety of ways. As they are sometimes a channel of communication between young people and local authorities, they can use the charter as a lobbying tool to ensure that the interests and needs of young people are being taken into account by these authorities. This can be an efficient method, especially at local level, where the authorities are in quite close contact with citizens and local networks.

The organisations can also implement the charter's principles in their everyday work which means, in practice, being more open to forming partnerships with young people and to taking their opinions on board. This does not imply that young people should become managers or board members (although this is possible), but is about creating a partnership where the roles, tasks and responsibilities are negotiated, agreed upon and accepted by all sides.

### *Local authorities*

By shaping local policies, managing local resources and looking for ways to improve the quality of community members' lives, the local authorities play a critical and unique role in creating the conditions necessary for young people to participate. The local authorities are also "closest to young people", so they have a responsibility to provide access to active citizenship and local democratic participation. Moreover, they have local knowledge and access to local networks that can support youth involvement in a variety of ways.

The charter provides a framework for a local approach to youth issues. It can also be seen as a tool to create or improve local youth policies that will support the involvement of young people in decision making and the development of

---

33. Examples are research agencies, networks of experts and specialists, education institutions, rehabilitation centres, etc.

different norms and practices affecting the young population in a community. For that reason the relevant measures that have been proposed in the charter should be implemented to the greatest possible extent (depending on the circumstances, resources available, past experience, etc.). Local authorities should be committed to underpinning young people's participation not only in governing processes at a local level, but also in a social environment – in schools, clubs, organisations, etc. Therefore, the measures promoted by the charter address both dimensions of youth participation, as they are interrelated and equally important for the benefit of the whole community.

### *How can different actors use the charter? – Review*

The list below is a collection of ideas that can inspire different actors to take action and to start using the charter as a tool in their everyday work. It is not a complete list – everybody should choose the actions that are the most relevant to their local needs and situations.

|  | **If you are a young person** | **If you are a representative of an organisation** | **If you are a representative of local authorities** |
|---|---|---|---|
| **Why should you use the charter?** | – to improve the situation of young people in your community<br>– to meet the needs of young people<br>– to get to know your rights<br>– to gain access to resources<br>– to make the voice of young people heard and be taken into consideration<br>– to influence the life of your local community<br>– to find out ways for constructive co-operation with local authorities<br>– to develop interaction between different actors in order to achieve your goals<br>– to use your skills and talents for the benefit of the others<br>– to contribute to the life of your community<br>– to gain new skills<br>– to gain useful experience<br>– to learn how local democracy works | – to improve the situation of young people in your community<br>– to meet the needs of young people<br>– to represent the interests of young people more efficiently<br>– to empower young people to participate<br>– to create new ways for young people to participate<br>– to create a more favourable work environment<br>– to fulfil the organisation's mission statement and aims<br>– to benefit from co-operation with local authorities<br>– to develop interaction between different actors in order to achieve your goals<br>– to gain useful experience | – to improve the situation of young people in your community<br>– to get to know and to meet the needs of young people<br>– to recognise and to value the role of young people<br>– to make better and more informed decisions<br>– to be more representative<br>– to create space for young people to contribute to the common good<br>– to create space for young people to practice democracy<br>– to find other ways of interacting with young people and youth organisations<br>– to benefit from co-operation with young people and organisations<br>– to develop local youth policy<br>– to improve your public image |

| How can you use the charter? | – to find out the areas in which you can participate at a local level<br>– to formulate the needs of young people in your local community, using the charter as a basis<br>– to inform the local actors about the existence of the charter and its content<br>– to promote the youth-friendly version of the charter in schools, clubs and youth groups<br>– to lobby the national representatives to the Congress of Local and Regional Authorities of the Council of Europe to disseminate the charter and good practices related to the charter<br>– to lobby youth organisations and local authorities to implement the recommendations of the charter<br>– to use the charter to lobby local authorities on policy issues<br>– to use the charter as a "passport" to ensure your participation in projects and initiatives<br>– to undertake research into the local situation<br>– to initiate and implement youth participation projects based on the RMSOS approach | – to formulate the needs of young people in your local community, using the charter as a basis<br>– to inform the local actors about the existence of the charter and its content<br>– to lobby the local authorities to implement the recommendations of the charter<br>– to develop positions on local issues<br>– to influence local youth policy<br>– to disseminate the charter and good practices related to the charter among interested parties<br>– to build partnerships with like-minded organisations in order to achieve your aims to lobby the national representatives to the Congress of Local and Regional Authorities of the Council of Europe<br>– to incorporate the principles promoted in the charter into different areas of work, into your mission statement, aims, priorities and policies<br>– to involve young people in decision-making processes<br>– to initiate and implement youth participation projects based on the RMSOS approach<br>– to use the charter as a training instrument for youth participation | – to do proper research on the situation of young people in the local context in order to properly assess what major challenges need to be addressed<br>– to develop services more responsive to the needs of young people<br>– to implement the measures proposed in the charter<br>– to use the charter as a reference point when developing a cross-sectoral local youth policy<br>– to incorporate the values and principles promoted in the charter into different areas of work<br>– to involve young people in making decisions that affect their lives (for example, by practising the co-management system)<br>– to support various forms of youth participation<br>– to create consultative bodies on issues related directly to youth<br>– to build local systems and structures for participation<br>– to monitor the degree of participation at a local level |
|---|---|---|---|

| What advantages and strengths do you already have? | – belonging to the local community<br>– being a large part of a local population<br>– knowing the local situation very well<br>– being motivated to improve the situation of young people<br>– being open to co-operate and to learn<br>– being willing to experiment<br>– having talents and potential that should be used for the benefit of the community | – having experience in undertaking participatory work<br>– being a channel for participation for young people<br>– being a part of the local context<br>– knowing the local situation very well<br>– sometimes being a link between young people and local authorities<br>– being a part of local networks<br>– having access to resources<br>– having information about where to get extra resources | – being close to young people<br>– knowing the local situation (political, social, economic, etc.)<br>– knowing local networks and initiatives and being part of them<br>– having access to resources<br>– having information about where to get extra resources<br>– having power and legitimacy to establish local rules<br>– having decision-making power to influence the local situation |
|---|---|---|---|

| **What do you need to be able to use the charter in the most efficient way?** | - to know that the charter exists and what its legal status is<br>- to develop the knowledge, skills and competencies necessary to participate at a local level<br>- to develop skills and competencies necessary to work with other age groups<br>- to gain skills for effective lobbying and advocacy<br>- to gain knowledge about the mechanisms of local democracy<br>- to understand local decision-making processes and the areas of responsibility of different actors<br>- to know how to use the charter<br>- to get training on how to implement the charter<br>- to gain moral and practical support from different actors<br>- to have a positive attitude towards working with adults and local authorities<br>- to develop strategies to access different resources<br>- to have self-confidence | - to know that the charter exists and what its legal status is<br>- to identify and develop new ways of working and functioning that are more "youth-friendly"<br>- to have relevant long-term policies in place<br>- to have a positive attitude towards local authorities<br>- to develop skills and competencies necessary to facilitate participation at a local level<br>- to develop skills and competencies necessary to work with young people<br>- to develop skills and competencies necessary to work with local authorities<br>- to get training on how to implement the charter<br>- to find examples of how the charter has been used in other communities or regions<br>- to develop strategies to access different resources | - to know that the charter exists and what its legal status is<br>- to have the political will for a long-term commitment to youth issues<br>- to be aware of the importance of youth participation<br>- to have a positive attitude towards young people and their capabilities<br>- to identify new ways of working and functioning that are more "youth-friendly"<br>- to develop skills and competencies necessary to work with young people<br>- to get training on how to implement the charter<br>- to find examples of how the charter has been used in other communities or regions<br>- to be willing to share the decision making in some fields<br>- to have different resources available<br>- to have relevant long-term policies in place<br>- to accept the work on youth participation as a challenge |

In order to use the charter in an effective way, all groups and actors need certain skills, knowledge, abilities and the right attitude, examples of which have been mentioned above. These are, however, only examples, and are aimed at helping groups and actors to identify what skills they still might need to acquire in order to use the recommendations of the charter in the best way.

> *Reflection time*
> 1. What benefits from implementing the charter would you expect to see in your community or organisation?
> 2. Which of the actions or ideas listed in the above chart should be undertaken in your local environment?

## 4.2. How to use the charter in practice?

### a. The six-step-model

The charter is a dynamic tool and can be used in many ways in various environments. There is no one universal model that would work in every town, region and country throughout Europe. It is therefore the role of local authorities, organisations and young people interested in youth participation at a local level to identify possible ways of using the charter in their own contexts, depending on their needs, situation, resources, etc.

There is, however, a model that can be helpful in providing general guidance on how to identify the practical measures needed in order to implement the recommendations of the revised charter in a local community. The model consists of six steps and ideally should be used by local authorities, organisations and young people working together on increasing youth participation.

The six-step process described below can be initiated in any community in Europe but needs good preparation in terms of:

- identifying the groups or actors who should participate;
- clarifying the actors' intentions and their motivation;
- information provided about what, when, how and with whom the process will take place;
- understanding the importance of youth participation, its benefits and limitations;
- development of the necessary skills; namely the skills required to perform social analysis, planning, communication and decision making, etc.;
- establishing partnerships in which everybody knows what his/her role is and knows exactly how he/she can contribute to the process;
- securing the necessary resources such as time, meeting facilities and possibly finance (for travel reimbursement, for example).

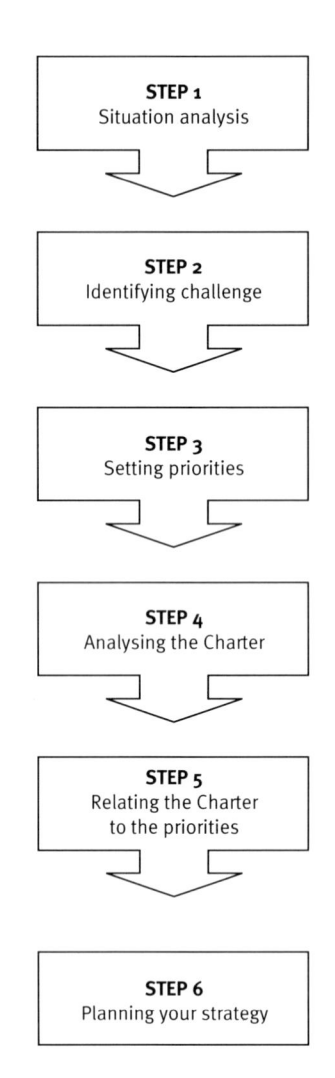

**Step 1 – What is the situation of young people in your region/town/village/area?**

Local actors are very familiar with the situation in their own community and environment and they know the factors affecting the involvement of young people. But because each actor perceives the situation from his/her own individual point of view, it is necessary to sit around a table and exchange views and opinions on what really is going on in a town or village. Perceptions of reality can often be very different and this stage requires enough time and special tools (such as methods and techniques used for social analysis) or even outside expertise, so that all the actors can better understand the views of the others before moving on to the next stage. Situation analysis can be done through observation and the analysis of experience, but it may sometimes be necessary to ask an external body or person, not involved in local issues on an everyday basis, to do some research.

**Step 2 – What are the opportunities, challenges and obstacles facing young people?**

An analysis of the situation of young people in the local environment is necessary in order to identify the most significant problems that they face. These can be directly related to youth participation (very limited opportunities to participate in cultural activities or lack of resources, for example), or they can be other factors that seem to have no direct link with participation, such as budget cuts in the local community.

**Step 3 – What should the priorities be?**

In general, young people face many challenges and problems and it is not possible to deal with all of them at the same time. That is why, in the short term, the local actors should decide on priority areas, those that need to be addressed first, especially if the resources available are limited. This might, in itself, be a demanding process, as different actors may have different views on what should be addressed first and why. For this reason, the situation analysis should be taken seriously, thus making the identification of priorities easier.

**Step 4 – What does the charter propose?**

Once the priority areas have been agreed upon, one can then refer to the charter to find the appropriate measures and practices to deal with the particular problems. These recommendations can be found in different parts of the charter, and so it is important to analyse not only the relevant part on sectoral policies, but also the recommendations concerning instruments and institutional participation.

**Step 5 – How does the charter relate to the priorities?**

At this stage, the actors need to identify exactly how the charter addresses the priority areas that were set in Step 3. Although the charter deals with a wide range of areas relating to youth involvement, there is a chance that the priority problems identified in Step 3 are not addressed, or are addressed only to a limited extent. In such cases, the actors are encouraged to look for other tools that might be available from different organisations or institutions active at regional, national or international levels.

> *Reflection time*
>
> 1. *What challenges faced by young people in your local context should be addressed first?*
> 2. *Why?*
> 3. *What measures does the charter propose in relation to the challenges you mentioned?*
> 4. *What principles promoted by the charter need to be respected when implementing the relevant recommendations?*
>
> *Suggestion: the above questions should first be answered by different actors and then the answers compared and discussed. In this way, it will be easier to see and understand the similarities and differences in perceptions, views and opinions.*

Remark

At this stage, it is important to mention that there is also another possible approach: that of first becoming familiar with the charter and then deciding which areas addressed in the charter are the most relevant. This would result in a different sequence of steps: Step 1 – getting to know the charter and its content; Step 2 – analysing the local situation in relation to the different areas of participation dealt with in the charter; Step 3 – identifying the most important challenges; Step 4 – setting priorities; Step 5 – relating the priorities to specific recommendations and measures proposed in the charter.

### Step 6 – How to plan the next steps using the charter

This is the last stage of the six-step-model, but in fact the first step in the process of implementing the charter to address the local situation. When the specific recommendations of the charter have been found, the actors need to discuss how they can actually implement these measures in their local context and need to plan exactly what should be done, where, how, by whom and with what resources. The charter leaves quite a lot of room for local actors to decide on how practices can be established or goals achieved, so that the most appropriate solutions can be found for each community or region.

### b. *RMSOS approach*

The charter can be used not only at the level of local policies or local decision making, but also within institutions or organisations and in the framework of youth projects, because it promotes values and principles strengthening meaningful youth participation. A tool to assess whether the right conditions for youth participation have been created is the RMSOS approach, already described in detail in Chapter 3 of this manual. This approach provides a framework that can help to discover whether young people have the right, means, space, opportunities and support within communities, organisations or projects – in other words, whether they have the elements necessary for their meaningful participation.

### c. *Participatory approach to planning youth projects*

Following the principles promoted by the charter in the field of project management is yet another way of using the charter in practice. Chapter 5 of this manual will describe in more detail how youth projects can be organised and implemented in order that more meaningful participation is possible.

# CHAPTER 5
## Youth participation projects

### 5.1. Managing youth participation projects

One of the key areas of youth participation is that of youth projects[34] organised for, with and by young people. In a local context, it is often the first opportunity for a young person to get involved in an activity that is beneficial not only for him/herself, but also for a wider group or community. Youth projects can therefore be a very important step for young people to experience how participation can work in reality.

> *Reflection time*
>
> 1. Are you involved in a youth project? In what capacity?
> 2. Is your project organised FOR young people?
> 3. Is your project organised WITH young people?
> 4. Is your project organised BY young people?
> 5. What are the consequences for your project of this FOR/WITH/BY young people?

*Participatory projects*

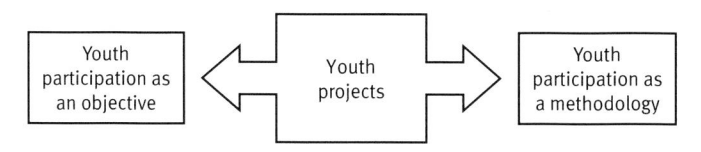

```
┌──────────────┐         ┌──────────┐         ┌──────────────┐
│    Youth     │         │          │         │    Youth     │
│participation │ <────── │  Youth   │ ──────> │participation │
│ as an        │         │ projects │         │ as a         │
│ objective    │         │          │         │ methodology  │
└──────────────┘         └──────────┘         └──────────────┘
```

*Dimensions of youth participation in youth projects*

Youth projects are an excellent way of enhancing the participation of young people at different levels, especially at local level. The diagram shows how the involvement of young people can be directly related to the aims and/or objectives of a project, but it can also be a strategy or methodology that is

---

34. See the definition of the term "project" in: "Project management T-kit", Council of Europe and European Commission, November 2000, pp. 27-29. Available at: www.training-youth.net/INTEGRATION/TY/Publications/tkits/tkit3/tkit3.pdf.

deliberately chosen in order to achieve the project's objectives. Ideally, both of these dimensions should be present for a project to be truly participatory in nature.

### Youth participation as a project aim and/or objective

In general, youth projects address a wide variety of issues or challenges that are often related directly or indirectly to participation, and they aim at achieving a situation where young people can have a bigger influence on decisions or actions affecting their lives. The projects can focus, for example, on empowering young people to participate (by skill or awareness development or by providing some information or tools, etc.), or they can focus on removing obstacles to youth participation, on building participation structures or infrastructure, or on setting up youth-adult partnerships, etc. A question remains, however, to what extent projects that focus exclusively on young people's hobbies (like playing computer games or collecting different items) can be seen as promoting meaningful youth participation.

### Youth participation as a project methodology

The "Project management T-kit", available from the Council of Europe, explains that the project methodology is the social, educational or organisational process through which the objectives will be pursued in a coherent manner; the way in which the different activities will build on each other in order to reach the objectives.[35] A methodology can also be described as an approach that guides the process of organising and running a project. Choosing a participatory approach to an activity has a number of very important effects on why, how, with whom and for whom a project is run. In practice, this means that the participants have a real influence on all the project elements and that ownership and decision-making power over different aspects is shared with or delegated completely to young people.

---

*Reflection time*

1. In what way is the dimension of youth participation as an objective present in your project?
2. In what way is the dimension of youth participation as methodology present in your project?
3. Can projects that focus exclusively on young people's hobbies (like playing computer games or collecting different items) be seen as promoting meaningful youth participation? What do you think?

---

### Values in participatory projects

Participatory youth projects are not value-free. A project organiser and all actors involved need to be aware of what they want and should ensure that meaningful participation of young people can be achieved. The main values that should be present in participatory projects are the following:

- mutual respect: accepting that other people (young people as well as adults) have the right to have different opinions and views;
- understanding cultural diversity: looking for constructive ways of dealing with differences that originate from the diversity of backgrounds;

---

35. Ibid., p. 56.

- promoting attitudes combating racism, extreme ideologies or xenophobia, so that young people can contribute to building more tolerant and peaceful societies;
- co-operation: different actors having an interest in youth participation should work together to achieve common goals and should provide mutual support;
- responsibility: all actors should take responsibility for co-operation and the results achieved;
- independence of young people: young people should have some autonomy within a project;
- inclusion of groups that have more difficulties in participating in public life due to their background, disabilities or other obstacles;
- gender equality: equal access to participation should be available for men and women;
- acknowledgement of the role of non-formal education as a tool to help young people participate;
- human rights approach;
- non-discriminatory approach.

*Participatory approach to project management*

Project management can be simply explained as the whole process of initiating, planning, implementing, evaluating and then closing down a project. When a project organiser chooses a methodology that is based on principles of meaningful participation, this implies that young people are involved in different aspects of managing the project; that they have power to influence decisions and processes and that they are granted the possibility to express their views and opinions. Youth can be involved in the management of the project in various roles and capacities, depending on what both sides have agreed.

> **Reflection time**
>
> 1. What are the values present in your project?
> 2. Who has determined them?
> 3. How are these values visible to the project actors and to the outside public?
> 4. Can you think of more values that are not listed here but seem relevant to you?

## 5.2. Step-by-step: planning and managing a youth project

A variety of models illustrating or structuring the process of preparing, running and evaluating a project exist. It is the responsibility of the person or team leading the project to choose the most appropriate model for a specific context taking into account the available resources. In recent years a model that has been used quite often in youth work is the one proposed in the "Project management T-kit".[36] It is therefore this model that will be used as a starting point for further reflection.

---

36. Ibid., p. 43.

> *Your task:*
>
> 1. Become familiar with the "Project management T-kit".
>
> In particular, read Chapter 3 entitled "The project: step-by-step".
>
> 2. Think of a project that you want to work on.

### Step 1 – Getting to know the local community and situation

Youth projects take place in a specific community and they aim at creating very concrete and visible social change. Before any project can start, it is therefore necessary to find out more about the situation and main challenges for young people within this community. Knowing the potential opportunities and concerns of the local population in a specific community will be very helpful in assessing the needs of the young people living there, as well as the needs of the community as a whole.

> *Reflection time (related to Step 1)*
>
> 1. What is the situation of young people in your local context (percentage of the population, background, financial situation, schooling, free-time activities, etc.)?
> 2. What kind of youth policy exists and is implemented in your community?
> 3. What are the opportunities for young people to participate in the life of your community?
> 4. What youth projects or initiatives are currently run in your community? By whom?
> 5. What is your relationship to the young people in your community (are you a youth leader, social worker, person responsible for youth issues in the local authorities, etc.)?

### Step 2.a – Needs analysis

Youth projects can be organised for a variety of reasons, but these reasons should relate to a large extent to the needs of young people and the needs of the local community in general. It is not enough just to want to organise something! If a project is to bring real change, it needs to address specific problems or deficits experienced at the local level, and the task of a project leader is to identify these challenges and to decide which ones should be addressed by the project. In order to recognise local needs it is therefore necessary to go through a "needs analysis" that "includes the social, political and economic conditions existing in the area of the project that make the project necessary".[37] Although project organisers sometimes underestimate or even neglect this step, it is in fact one of the most important in the whole process of project preparation, because it indicates what the aim of the project should be. Numerous methods and techniques exist to help identify local needs. Examples are observations, interviews, surveys, focus groups, scenario analyses and many more, and it is the task of a project organiser to choose the most appropriate method according to the type of information needed and the resources and expertise available. In the case of local youth projects, where the resources are usually very limited, project organisers often use the simplest methods to analyse local needs and, in most cases, these are more than sufficient as long as several parties are involved in the whole process.

---

37. Ibid., p. 46.

> *Reflection time (related to Step 2.a)*
>
> 1. What are the main challenges that young people face in your community, especially in the field of participation in local life? What causes them?
> 2. How do you know about them? What is your source of information?
> 3. What has been already done to strengthen youth participation at the local level? What are the results?
> 4. What more do young people wish to do to strengthen their participation in local life?
> 5. To what extent is your local community interested in supporting this?
> 6. What does your project aim to change for the young people in question?
> 7. Why is your project important for young people and the whole community?

### Step 2.b – Institutional analysis

Youth projects are usually prepared and run by groups, organisations or institutions that are related in one way or another to youth work. Although projects should address local needs and should contribute to a social change, they should also be appropriate to the institution concerned, to its values and priorities. Running a project within the framework of an institution can bring many benefits, such as using the existing experience, facilities and infrastructure or other resources, but it can also generate a lot of difficulties. That is why before starting a project it is important to ask a number of questions that can help to find out how the project and the institution fit together. This is called an "institutional analysis".

> *Reflection time (related to Step 2.b)*
>
> 1. What is the connection between young people and the institution running the project?
> 2. Is youth participation an important value for this institution? How do you know this?
> 3. How can young people get involved in the work of this institution (not only in the framework of the project proposed, but also in other fields)?
> 4. What would be the role of the institution in the project?
> 5. What benefits and risks does your project bring to this institution?

### Step 2.c – Personal motivation

Different motivations are involved in the organisation of a youth project. It has been already mentioned that the most important motivation should relate to some local need or the needs of young people, but the motivation of individuals working on a project also plays a very important role, since project organisers have an enormous influence on different aspects of their project.

> *Reflection time (related to Step 2.c)*
>
> 1. *Why is youth participation important for you?*
> 2. *Why are you personally interested in organising this project? What do you think you will gain?*
> 3. *Is your motivation for undertaking this project in line with the motivation of your institution?*
> 4. *What is your experience and expertise in the field of youth participation?*

## Step 3 – Defining aims

The previous steps provide an explanation of the situation in a local community and why a project is necessary in that specific context. The next step is to define the purpose of the project and what it is hoped to achieve, especially over the long term. The aims usually consist of an ideal situation in which the project achieves absolutely everything expected of it and the planned social change happens in reality. Aims are often rather general in nature, so at the end of a project it is very difficult or even impossible to measure to what extent they have been achieved. Even so, they give a sense of direction throughout the whole project. Some project managers say that a good description of a project's aims is, in fact, rather like a very short project summary in that it highlights the most important aspects of the project. The aims are an element of the project that cannot change – if they do change it means that a new project has been created. What can change, however, are the objectives or specific methods involved.

> *Reflection time (related to Step 3)*
>
> 1. *What does your project intend to change in the field of youth participation of young people in your local community?*
> 2. *Who should be involved in the project (which actors)?*
> 3. *Who will benefit from the project and in what way(s)?*
> 4. *What is the geographical scope of the project?*
> 5. *Optional: how are you going to do this? (This is not a question about activities or methods, but about methodology.)*

## Step 4 – Formulating objectives

Because the aims of a project remain rather general and it is not always possible to measure to what extent they have been achieved, it is necessary to formulate more concrete goals or objectives. These will show the project organisers and the actors what they need to do in order to achieve the social change they are aiming at. Objectives need to be as concrete as possible, so that it is clear to all involved what actions are necessary and it can be easily checked whether or not an action has been completed. There are different ways of formulating project objectives and one method goes under the acronym "SMART". The objectives are SMART if they are:

- Specific: they state precisely what one intends to do or achieve;
- Measurable: it is possible to check if they have been met and to what extent;
- Achievable: the project does not attempt too much;
- Realistic: they can be achieved within the existing context and with the existing resources;
- Timed: they state when the objectives will be fulfilled.

> *Reflection time (related to Step 4)*
>
> 1. What precisely will be done to meet the needs of young people targeted by your project?
> 2. How realistic are these objectives?
> 3. How and when can you check if the planned actions have taken place?
> 4. How will these actions contribute to achieving the overall aim of the project?
> 5. How will you empower young people to take an active role in your project?

## Step 5 – Choosing the methodology

It has been already explained what a project methodology is and how important it is when organising a project on youth participation. One should not confuse "methodology" and "methods", however, because methods are concrete tools or ways of doing things (such as some types of activities or exercises). When planning the methodology of a participatory project, it is very important to ensure that:

- young people have ownership of the project;
- young people understand what the project is about and what it wants to achieve;
- young people can influence different elements of the project;
- young people have responsibilities within the project;
- young people have meaningful tasks to perform;
- young people have space to express their opinions and views about the project;
- young people have an opportunity to learn the skills necessary to participate in the project;
- young people are treated as project partners, not as objects or victims;
- the types of activities run within the project are suitable for young people.

> *Reflection time (related to Step 5)*
>
> 1. How would you describe the methodology of your project?
> 2. To what extent does this methodology create a space for the meaningful participation of young people?
> 3. What is your experience in working with a methodology focusing on youth participation?
> 4. Do you need to develop special skills or competencies to work more efficiently with such a methodology? What are these?
> 5. Where can you get the necessary support to gain these skills and competencies?

## Step 6 – Making a plan of activities

This is the moment in the process of project preparation when a plan of all the activities that will take place within the project framework can be formed. At this stage, it is useful to prepare a list of tasks that need to be accomplished for each activity, so that all stakeholders are clear about the amount of work necessary. This can also help to make a realistic estimation of the time (and other resources, such as finance, for example) that will be needed. The place of activities within a project is sometimes compared to an iceberg, as it is only this part of the project that is visible to the public eye. The whole process of project preparation is, however, much broader, and includes many tasks and steps that might be visible only to the parties directly involved.

*Project iceberg*

---

***Reflection time (related to Step 6)***

1. *What is the flow of activities within your project?*
2. *When exactly do they take place? Where and with whom do they take place? Is everything planned in such a way that it ensures meaningful participation of young people?*
3. *Who should be responsible for carrying out specific activities?*
4. *In what way do the activities relate to each other?*
5. *How does each activity relate to the objectives of the whole project?*
6. *Are all the objectives linked to activities in your project?*
7. *Is your plan achievable and realistic? Why do you think so?*

### Step 7 – Implementing activities

Once the planning has been done, it is time to start work and to move forward in order to achieve the desired results. When one speaks of "implementing activities" one does not only mean management of the project, but also fulfilment of all the different tasks needed in order to prepare the activities and to close them down. Such tasks include:

- managing the people involved and making sure that their talents and strengths are used efficiently;
- encouraging young people to take on responsibilities and tasks within the project;
- managing other resources available (finances, infrastructure, know-how, time, etc.);
- taking daily decisions related to different aspects of the project;
- making sure that things happen according to plan;
- evaluating different aspects of the project on a regular basis;
- ensuring good co-operation with and among young people;
- adjusting the project to new circumstances if necessary;
- dealing with unexpected developments and factors that cannot be controlled by a project manager.

> *Reflection time (related to Step 7)*
>
> 1. Who is going to be responsible for implementation of the overall project?
> 2. What are the roles of different actors (for example, the young people involved)? Are they all clear about their roles and what is expected of them?
> 3. Do the actors have enough competencies and skills to implement the project? What kinds of support will they need and how can this support be ensured?
> 4. What are the resources needed to implement your project?
> 5. Where will you obtain these resources?

## Step 8 – Evaluating

Before a project can be closed down, there needs to be an evaluation in order to find out to what extent the objectives have been fulfilled and how the project process worked, so that recommendations can be made for similar initiatives in the future. An evaluation is often perceived as something negative – a list of the things that did not work. It is therefore important to plan it carefully, so that it becomes an opportunity to make a good quality assessment that will highlight the project's achievements as well as its weaknesses. Young people should be active participants in an evaluation and this can be achieved by applying a participatory approach to project evaluation.

Participatory evaluation should be based on the following principles:

- the evaluation process provides space for young people to take responsibility for meaningful tasks;
- young people are clear about their role in the evaluation;
- young people are aware of what evaluation is;
- the evaluation is planned together with young people;
- young people need to have the necessary support to be able to play a meaningful role in the evaluation process;
- the views and opinions of young people have the same value as those of adults;
- the evaluation is useful to young people;
- the evaluation focuses on the present, past and future of the project.

> *Reflection time (related to Step 8)*
>
> 1. What is the purpose of evaluation for your project?
> 2. Which aspects and dimensions of the project do you plan to evaluate?
> 3. How are you going to do this? Are you planning to use some specific evaluation techniques and methods? Which ones and why these?
> 4. To what extent did young people participate in the planning of the evaluation?
> 5. What is the role of young people in the evaluation process? Has this role been agreed/negotiated with them?
> 6. What are the needs of young people in relation to evaluation competencies and how are you going to meet these needs?
> 7. What is your expertise and experience in running a participatory evaluation?

*Step 9 – Follow-up*

Youth projects aim at creating a positive change in a local context, so that once a project has been successfully completed, the local community and/or young people can clearly see a development or change in the life of the community. Ideally, this will mean that the results of the project will be sustained over the long term.

> *Reflection time (related to Step 9)*
> 1. *How are you going to ensure that the results of your project will be long lasting?*
> 2. *Who needs to be involved in this follow-up and how will you ensure this involvement?*
> 3. *What will be the role of young people in securing the continuity of the project achievements?*

## 5.3. Quality criteria for participatory projects

There is no ready-to-use recipe that gives step-by-step instructions on how to organise a perfect participatory project, since the situations in different parts of Europe or even within one country are very different. Such a recipe can, however, be created by and for specific communities, groups or organisations, so that it fits those particular situations and addresses their most important needs. Creating a recipe means, in practice, deciding how much of each ingredient one needs to use and how to use it, in order that the desired dish can be prepared. In the case of participatory projects, the "quality criteria" play the role of ingredients, which can be mixed together in different combinations. Below is a list of criteria that can help to guide a project organiser in the process of creating a fully participatory project. The list is not exhaustive and other criteria can, of course, be added.

It needs to be decided to what extent criteria have been fulfilled by a project – with 0 indicating that a criterion has not been fulfilled at all, and 5 indicating that a criterion has been fully fulfilled. One can then, if necessary, plan how these criteria can be fulfilled to a greater extent. This exercise is intended to help in assessing existing projects and to be a tool for self-evaluation.

| Criteria related to the purpose of the project | Grade (0-5) | Justification of the grade |
|---|---|---|
| The project aims at fulfilling the needs of young people | | |
| The aims and objectives of the project have been negotiated and agreed with young people | | |
| Young people are aware of possible benefits from participating in the project | | |

| Criteria related to project design | Grade (0-5) | Justification of the grade |
|---|---|---|
| Young people understand what the project is about | | |
| Information about the project is easily accessible for young people who might be interested in getting involved | | |
| The infrastructure necessary to support the participation of young people exists | | |
| The activities take place in a location accessible by young people | | |
| The activities take place at a time suitable for young people (and not during school hours, for example) | | |
| Project procedures and policies are comprehensible for young people | | |
| Documents related to the project are comprehensible for young people | | |
| The costs of participation in the project are reimbursed | | |
| The project design is flexible | | |

| Criteria related to different stages of the project | Grade (0-5) | Justification of the grade |
|---|---|---|
| Young people have been involved in initiating the project | | |
| Young people are involved in the preparation of the project | | |
| Young people are involved in disseminating information about the project | | |
| Young people are involved in the implementation of the project | | |
| Young people are involved in the evaluation of the project | | |
| Young people are involved in the follow-up of the project | | |

| Criteria related to accessibility of the project | Grade (0-5) | Justification of the grade |
|---|---|---|
| The project is open to all young people regardless of their gender, social class, resources, etc. | | |
| The project is open to young people who are not members of any formal youth structures | | |
| The project creates equal opportunities for men and women to participate | | |

| Criteria related to decision-making power | Grade (0-5) | Justification of the grade |
|---|---|---|
| Young people know what is expected of them | | |
| Young people are aware of responsibilities they have | | |
| The roles and tasks within the project are negotiated and agreed by young people and adults | | |
| Young people know the identities and roles of the actors involved in the project | | |
| Young people know how the decision-making process within the project functions | | |
| Young people are present at different decision-making levels in the project | | |
| Young people are regularly informed about the progress, successes, challenges and more important developments of the project | | |
| The views and opinions of young people have the same value as the views and opinions of adults | | |
| Young people have meaningful tasks and roles to fulfil | | |
| Young people have autonomy in fulfilling their tasks | | |
| The contribution of young people is recognised and valued | | |
| Young people have decision-making power within the project | | |

| Criteria related to support | Grade (0-5) | Justification of the grade |
|---|---|---|
| The institution running the project fully supports young people's involvement | | |
| A mentor or guarantor is available if young people need him/her | | |
| Special support is provided for disadvantaged and more vulnerable young people | | |
| Young people get support in developing project management skills | | |
| Young people get the support necessary for their involvement in decision making | | |
| Young people have a chance to learn from their own mistakes | | |
| Young people are aware of what skills and competencies they need to develop in order to fully participate in the project | | |

*Reflection time*

1. *Which of the above criteria have to be fulfilled so that we can talk about a "participatory project"?*
2. *Which of the above criteria would you consider "desirable" (as opposed to essential) for a participatory project?*

# CHAPTER 6
## Co-operation at a local level

### 6.1. Getting ready for co-operation

Co-operation between local authorities, youth and their organisations is a necessary step in building strong and democratic communities. As experience shows, such co-operation might be quite a challenge, but there are many examples of constructive ways in which different actors from the local scene can work together to achieve common goals.

Various parties seek co-operation when they have similar interests and when they see benefits from working together, and it is therefore essential to discover what areas of mutual interest exist between local authorities and young people or their organisations. Ideally, all partners will communicate their needs and goals in an open and honest manner, so that the basis for further co-operation can be agreed upon. If contradictory goals have been identified, they need to be addressed as soon as possible, otherwise co-operation may be hindered or even blocked at a later stage. Different methods can be used to find out the interests of each side. In some communities, meetings are arranged in which these issues are discussed between potential partners, in others an expert is given the responsibility to identify these interests on the basis of research. This can be analysis of the priorities and policies of communities and organisations, taking account of various reports and other political documents, and can be the analysis of actions and projects.

Examples of young people's interest in co-operating with other actors are:
- improving the situation of young people in the community;
- contributing to the improvement of the general situation in the local community;
- representing the interests of young people in the decision-making process;
- having an influence on local decisions and policies;
- having their opinions heard;
- gaining access to resources;
- getting new opportunities in life;
- making new contacts;
- gaining access to networks;
- using their potential, talents and skills;
- using their time in a useful way;
- gaining new experience.

Examples of youth organisations' interest in co-operating with other actors are:

- improving the situation of young people in the community;
- contributing to the improvement of the general situation in the local community;
- representing the interests of young people in the decision-making process;
- having an influence on local decisions and policies;
- building good relations with the parties that have decision-making power;
- being visible in a local context;
- creating a good impression of the organisation in a local context;
- advertising their activities;
- gaining access to resources;
- gaining access to services;
- sharing their experience for the benefit of others;
- fulfilling an organisation's aims and objectives;
- creating participation frameworks and structures at local level;
- educating, providing experience and preparing young people for their future lives;
- gaining new experience.

Examples of local authorities' interest in co-operating with other actors are:

- contributing to the improvement of the general situation in the local community;
- identifying the needs of young people more accurately;
- providing better services to young people;
- improving the situation of young people in the local context;
- preventing social problems;
- implementing their plans and political priorities;
- creating ownership of decisions among those affected by them;
- getting feedback on proposals and ideas;
- preparing young people for future responsibilities (in terms of community management, for example);
- being visible in the local context;
- creating a good impression of the local authorities in the community
- political reasons (being re-elected?).

When the common interests have been agreed upon, the parties can start to look for possible areas of co-operation. The revised charter mentions, for example, the areas of youth unemployment, education, health, gender equality and sustainable development, etc. It also contains concrete examples of initiatives or actions that can be jointly undertaken by different actors in the local scene.

The co-operation can take place in different areas and also at different levels. In some communities, partnerships are created to address specific local problems (limited access to culture, for example) or to implement specific policies (such as the local policy to combat alcohol and drug addiction). In other communities, co-operation is established at the level of decision making, so that young people and their organisations are invited to take part in governing meetings that influence policies or at which decisions affecting them are taken. The final level at which co-operation is established is the result of negotiation, so that the needs and interests of each party can be fulfilled. Consequently, although co-operation between local actors may take different forms, the main aim remains the same – strong partnerships contribute to building better lives in local communities.

> *Reflection time*
>
> 1. What interests would motivate you to start co-operation with another party? (If you represent a youth organisation, this would be co-operation with local authorities vice versa);
> 2. What could be examples of contradictory interests of local authorities and youth organisations? Have you ever been in a situation where contradictory interests were represented? How was it dealt with?
> 3. Which areas of co-operation mentioned in the charter would be the most relevant in your local community? Why?(Refer to Part I of the charter dealing with sectoral policies.

The remainder of this chapter will give details of specific forms of co-operation between local authorities and youth organisations and young people.

## 6.2. Co-operation in the area of decision making – Consultation model

Consultation is one of the mechanisms that can be used efficiently in order to involve young people in decision making at a local level. Various definitions of what consultation means exist, depending on the form it takes, the goals it seeks to achieve, the distribution of authority between different parties, etc. Consultation with young people can be explained as a way of collecting their views and opinions, or obtaining feedback relating to actions or proposals affecting them. Meaningful consultation is a two-way process and takes place when it is still possible to influence the final outcome or what is going to happen.

Consultation is perceived as a process in which the power and the final say rests with adults. This means that although young people get an opportunity to contribute and to express their views, at the end the adults have the power to decide if and to what extent these contributions will be used.

There is an ongoing debate between practitioners and researchers about the benefits and limitations of consultation. It has been questioned whether it is an appropriate way of involving young people in the decision-making process in the public domain, and it is has been suggested that there is a real risk of a "tokenistic" approach to consultation in some contexts.

A review of arguments for and against consultation of young people:[38]

---

38. Adapted from: McAuley, K. and Brattman, M., *Hearing young voices. Executive summary,* Open Your Eyes to Child Poverty Initiative, Ireland, 2002, p. 13.

| In favour of consultation | Against consultation |
|---|---|
| Young people have a right to be heard and to influence decisions important to them | Young people need to learn responsibility before they can be granted rights |
| The above-mentioned right to be heard can protect young people, as the adults do not always speak in the best interests of young people | Adults know what young people need and should exercise their right to speak on behalf of young people |
| All the institutions whose work has an impact on the lives of young people should have dialogue with these young people | The interests of young people are represented by organisations working with young people, so there is no need for direct contact |
| Giving no opportunities for young people to present their views shows a lack of respect and recognition of young people and their capabilities | Asking young people to express their ideas on serious issues means that young people are forced to play adult roles before they are ready to do so |
| Young people have the freedom to decide if they want to exercise the right to express their opinions or not | Young people do not want to be consulted |
| Consulting youth will lead to improved decisions, as young people can make meaningful contributions when they are allowed to do so | Young people lack the maturity, knowledge and skills to make meaningful contributions, especially in respect of decision making at a public policy level |
| Existing decision-making structures should be adapted to accommodate consultation with young people | It is not possible to accommodate consultation with young people within existing decision-making structures |
| Expressing ideas and being heard is a part of every citizen's education and strengthens commitment to democracy | Giving young people an opportunity to speak and be heard can undermine their respect for adult authority |
| Having a say and being heard will encourage young people to be active citizens in the future | Young people are not interested in politics and public policy |
| Young people are more likely to respect and follow decisions if they are involved in making them | There are insufficient resources available |
|  | There are no structures and guidelines to support consultation |

Even if views on the value of consultation differ, it is still seen in many institutions as a valuable way of bringing young people's insights into decision-making processes and as a tool for ensuring social inclusion (when consulting socially excluded youth).

> *Reflection time*
>
> 1. *Have you ever taken part in consultation? In what context?*
> 2. *What do you think – should young people be consulted in the public decision-making domain? Why?*
> 3. *Do you agree with the statement: "Asking young people to express their ideas on serious issues means that young people are forced to play adult roles before they are ready to do so"? Why? Explain your point of view.*

Ideally, a consultation process should be based on the following principles:

– *Adults understand the importance and benefits of consulting youth*

Consultation should be initiated and run by those who believe in the value of this form of co-operation, and who are aware of its benefits and limitations. Otherwise the whole process might result in a "tokenistic" initiative.

– *Young people need to be enabled to make a contribution*

Young people have a lot of potential and talent, but they might be lacking the knowledge or skills to make a meaningful contribution. It is the responsibility of adults to make sure that young people are empowered and enabled to gain these knowledge or skills.

– *Young people are involved in preparing and running consultation*

Young people are capable of taking responsibility and contributing to the whole process of organising consultation. As a result, they feel that they are "owners" of the resulting decisions and can gain valuable experience in different aspects of local democracy.

– *The consultation has a clear purpose and the participants are informed about it*

Young people should know why consultation is taking place and what will happen as a result of it, namely to what extent these results will influence the final decision. This can help them to form realistic expectations about what can be achieved.

– *Young people are informed about how the whole consultation process works*

Consultation processes can be constructed in different ways and young people need to know at which stage this specific consultation process is and what still has to happen.

– *Young people should be consulted as early on in the decision-making process as possible*

The aim of consultation should be to hear the voice of young people in relation to proposals or decisions affecting their lives, in order that the proposals can be adjusted to their needs and views. If the consultation process takes place during the final stages of the decision-making process, there is little space for young people to have any influence on the final shape of the proposal.

– *The right methodologies should be chosen*

The methodology of consultation should be appropriate to the age, background, education level, etc. of the young people concerned. Thus it might be a good idea to involve facilitators who have experience in working with youth in order to make sure that the items are presented in such a way that young people can understand and will feel motivated to work on them.

– *Recommendations of young people are seriously considered*

Consultation should not take place if its results remain only on paper. The results need to be analysed and discussed to identify the best ways of using them. Consultation with local youth can bring very valuable ideas and feedback and the party organising the consultation should make use of this. In some communities, a senior representative from the local authorities is present during the consultation process to ensure that its results can be heard at the highest level. Practitioners working in this field indicate that young people need tangible evidence that their views have been taken on board and it is therefore important that at least some of the proposals are implemented.[39] This will ensure the future involvement of young people in similar initiatives.

– *There is adequate time allocated for consultation*

Consultation is a time-consuming process. It needs preparation and enough time for young people to express their views. That is why the timing of the whole process should be well planned so that meaningful contributions can be gathered. If young people need more time to develop their ideas, opportunities for further consultation should be created.

– *The consultation is held at a time appropriate for young people and in a place that is accessible to them*

Time and location of consultation play important roles in involving young people. If the venue is difficult to reach then transport should be provided or the travel costs should be reimbursed. In some cases more than one consultation venue can be used so that even more young people get a chance to have their say.

– *The consultation is run in a setting that will encourage young people to contribute*

Although the issue presented to young people can be of the highest importance, it is nevertheless crucial to create conditions in which young people feel comfortable and secure about sharing their ideas. To help this process, some organisations try to hold consultations in informal settings.

– *Young people are informed about the result of consultation*

Even if it is some time after the consultation, young people have a right to be informed about the outcome and about the ways in which their contribution has had an effect (specifically the ways in which proposals or decisions changed or not, as the case may be).

– *The views and opinions of young people are respected and valued*

Young people want to contribute and share their views, but they also need to know that this contribution is important for the local community. It is not enough to declare that young people's views are respected This should also be demonstrated by recording the information received from them so that their views can be accurately presented to other parties and also by avoiding making of paternalistic comments such as "what do these young people know about real life?", etc.

– *The contribution of young people is acknowledged and recognised*

Recognising the contribution of young people is a way of saying "thank you" to them and of motivating them to get involved in future initiatives. A number of methods can be used for this purpose, for example:

- articles or reports in local or regional media (local newspapers, radio, etc.);
- provision of certificates;
- provision of personal references;
- sending thank you letters;
- covering the costs related to consultation;
- provision of food;
- provision of small souvenirs;
- invitations to a social event;
- invitations to join decision-making or consultation bodies at a local level;
- pocket money (although this is considered to be controversial).

---

39. McAuley, K. and Brattman, M., op. cit., p. 11.

> *Reflection time*
> 1. Which principles of consultation are, in your opinion, the most important? Why?
> 2. What could make the consultation process more attractive for young people?
> 3. What do you think about rewarding young people who participate in consultations with pocket money?
> 4. Would you add any principles to the ones mentioned above?

Consultation can be organised in a variety of ways. Direct consultation involves direct contact with young people living in a specific community or region and can take the form of:

- holding consultation meetings or events at which young people can learn more about the issue or proposal and where they can express their views;
- holding consultation events with under-represented youth;
- holding consultation events in a school setting;
- inviting views by sending e-mails, letters, essays, etc.;
- inviting views by creating a piece of art: a drawing, sculpture, poem, etc.;
- individual or group interviews;
- questionnaires, self-completed surveys;
- referenda, polling;
- telephone surveys;
- comment and/or complaint systems;
- a neighbourhood forum. A forum can be a group from a geographically defined area that meets regularly to discuss and analyse issues, plans and proposals. Membership can be fixed or open.

In some cases, however, indirect consultation can be more appropriate, either because there are not enough resources available or because the group of young people is very large, thereby making it difficult to reach all of them. This can be done by:

- consulting groups of representatives. Ideally, young people themselves should decide who would represent them for a specific consultation. In reality, however, this is often hard to achieve, and therefore a minimum condition for working with such a group should be that it is representative of the local youth population. These groups of representatives are established for the purpose of consultation only;
- youth panels. These are panels of young people who are broadly representative of a specific community. They are usually larger groups whose members have a regular opportunity to meet (often twice a year) and share their views and ideas about the issues affecting the lives of young people in the community;
- consulting with existing groups of representatives. Young people elect their representatives to various councils and boards. As it is assumed that these bodies are representative of the local youth population, they are also asked for their views and contributions on behalf of all the young people in this community;

- creating focus groups. These groups are especially effective when there is little information available on a specific topic. The information is gathered during a group interaction that is facilitated by a moderator who runs a type of a group interview;[40]
- consulting experts. These experts are young people who develop expertise in particular fields. They are sometimes consulted when they have a good insight into the topic of the consultation, as they themselves represent young people;
- young citizen's jury.[41] These are made up of 6 to 20 young people who are called together to make a judgment on an important issue or proposal. Just as in a real court, they can ask witnesses, hear evidence, etc.

> *Reflection time*
>
> 1. What benefits and limitations of direct and indirect consultation can you see?
> 2. Give examples of potential items and questions relevant to the local community you represent, which could be addressed to young people in the form of direct consultation?
> 3. Give examples of potential items and questions relevant to the local community you represent, which could be addressed to young people in the form of indirect consultation?

The variety of forms that consultation can take at a local level ensures that this method of co-operation with young people can be used in very different contexts and situations. Consultation does not have to be a complicated initiative (unless its scope is very wide and complicated) and sometimes a simple, but well-prepared consultation meeting can generate very meaningful results.

### 6.3. Co-operation in the area of decision making – Committee model

The revised charter states that "effective participation of young people in local and regional affairs ... requires a permanent representative structure such as a youth council, a youth parliament or a youth forum".[42] The role of such a structure can vary from one community or region to the other, but it should always be a forum in which young people can freely express their opinions, concerns and proposals related to the policies and actions of local authorities in the area of youth work. A youth council or parliament should be a space where a meaningful dialogue and partnership between youth and local authorities can be created, so that all the actors involved can observe tangible benefits of such co-operation.

Young people are not the only ones who benefit from having a youth council or parliament. Thanks to these structures, local authorities can ensure true representation of the whole community (young people constituting a substantial part of the population) and can take decisions that are more relevant to the needs of the inhabitants. Young people also bring a different perspective when looking at local issues and through their involvement in local processes.

---

40. For more information about focus groups see: *Young voices. Guidelines on HOW to involve children and young people in your work*, The National Children's Office, Ireland, 2005.
41. For more information about citizen's juries see: *People & participation. How to put citizens at the heart of decision-making*, Involve, 2005.
42. The revised European Charter on the Participation of Young People in Local and Regional Life, Congress of Local and Regional Authorities of the Council of Europe, May 2003, III.1.59.

Structures representing youth at a local or regional level can take different forms and different names, depending on the context; they may be called "youth councils", "youth forums", "youth parliaments" or "youth boards", for example. For the purpose of this manual, such structures will be referred to as "committees", and will be defined as follows: "permanent structures of youth participation at a local level, representing the opinions and views of young people living in these communities or regions. In particular, the committees will represent young people's views on the policies and initiatives of different decision-making bodies, in cases where the policies have an effect on the lives of young people living in the community".

Members of youth committees can be appointed or elected and they can represent organisations, political parties or can be independent. Ideally, the composition of such a committee should reflect the sociological composition of the local community, so that less privileged groups also have an opportunity to be represented.

When setting up a local youth committee, the local authorities and young people or youth organisations need to reflect together on the following questions:

*Purpose of the committee*
- Why is such a committee needed in the local community?
- Who exactly should it represent?
- Who is interested in establishing it? Why? What is the motivation?
- What should be the committee's role?
- What should be its scope of interest?
- What should be its rights and responsibilities?
- What should be its relationship to local authorities?
- What decision-making power does the committee have?
- How will the local authorities view the committee's contributions?

*Committee composition*
- How many members should the committee have? Why?
- How can a gender, geographical or other relevant balance be achieved?
- How can the groups that are usually under-represented in decision-making bodies (such as handicapped people, minority representatives, etc.) be reached?
- Should any quota system (such as that based on age, gender, ethnic background, etc.) be introduced?

*Members' profile*
- Who can be a member? What should the criteria be?
- How old should they be?
- What skills and competencies do they need in order to have committee responsibility?

*Members' selection*
- How should committee members be selected? How should this work in practice? Is it realistic?
- Should there be a formal nomination? By whom?
- Who should be involved in recruitment?
- Where can potential candidates be found?
- How can potential candidates be motivated to become a candidate for the committee?

*Members' mandate*
- What responsibilities should committee members have?
- What should be their rights and privileges?
- How long would the term of office be? Can this term be renewed?
- Are any disciplinary measures needed?

*Members' empowerment*
- What knowledge and skills will the committee members need to have or develop?
- How can they do this?
- What support will the committee members need in order to fulfil their responsibilities?
- Who can provide such support?

*Structure of the committee*
- What should the functions and roles be within the committee?
- What bodies or sub-committees will be needed?
- Should the committee structure mirror that of local government? Why?
- How formal should the structure be?

*Mode of work*
- What will be working methods of the committee (for example, meetings, consultations, research, etc.)?
- How often should meetings be scheduled?
- Who will prepare and run the meetings?
- What work should take place in between the meetings?
- How will the decisions be made?
- Who will provide secretarial or administrative support?
- Are there any rules that need to be agreed upon?

*Co-operation with local authorities*
- What form should the co-operation take?
- How will information be exchanged?
- Should this be a regular exchange or on request?
- Who, in the committee, will be responsible for keeping in touch with local authorities?
- Who, in the local authorities, will be responsible for contact with the committee?
- What should be done in cases of disagreement between the parties?

*Staying in touch with local youth*
- How will the views of young people be represented in the work of the committee?
- How will the results of the committee's work, its successes and challenges, be communicated to local young people?
- In what way can other young people influence the work of the committee?

*Technical arrangements*
- Where will the committee be located (meeting place, working space, official address, etc.)?
- Who will cover the expenses?
- Should the members receive some pocket money or other incentives?

*Other*
- Should there be a constitution or other document regulating the most important aspects of committee procedure? Why?

The above list of questions is based on the experience of different groups that have already gone through the process of setting up a youth council or parliament at local level. The list is rather long and probably not very exciting either for young people or politicians alike, thus illustrating the dilemma of how to create a structure that can function efficiently on one hand and be youth-friendly on the other. Various groups have tried solutions such as eliminating the number of formal procedures, ensuring an informal and friendly work atmosphere and preparing documents in youth-friendly language, but it is still considered to be a real challenge to attract young people to this rather formal form of participation.

---

**Reflection time**

1. Is there a youth council or parliament or forum in your local community? What do you know about the way it operates?
2. What strengths and weaknesses of this form of co-operation between local authorities and young people do you see?
3. How can young people be motivated to join committees at a local level?

---

## 6.4. Co-operation in the area of decision making – Co-management

Co-management (or co-operative management) means the sharing of power, responsibility and accountability in the area of management, between two or more parties. This system can be used successfully when involving young people in decision-making processes at various levels. The Council of Europe introduced the co-management system over thirty years ago when it created a unique partnership between the representatives of youth organisations and governments within the Directorate of Youth and Sport. This system gives young people an opportunity to have their say in the formulation and implementation of the Council of Europe's youth policy.

### Co-management in the Council of Europe

The Directorate of Youth and Sport (DYS) of the Council of Europe provides guidelines and legal instruments that support the creation of youth policies at local, national and European levels. The most important decisions related to the programme and budgetary priorities are taken jointly by governmental and non-governmental partners in the framework of the co-management system.

There are four bodies involved in the DYS co-management system:

1. The European Steering Committee for Youth (CDEJ). Its members represent the ministries responsible for youth affairs from the member states of the Council of Europe, as well as other states that have subscribed to the European Cultural Convention. This committee ensures intergovernmental co-

operation in the field of youth and youth policies. It meets twice a year in plenary session and addresses youth-related issues and challenges.

2. The Advisory Council. It has 30 members representing international non-governmental youth organisations and networks, national youth committees properly constituted in Council of Europe member states (so-called National Youth Councils) and structures involved in various areas of youth work relevant to the Council of Europe's youth policy. The role of the Advisory Council is to promote non-governmental participation in decision-making processes in the youth sector of the Council of Europe.

3. The Joint Council on Youth. It consists of all members of the European Steering Committee for Youth and the Advisory Council and it is the main decision- and policy-making body for governmental and non-governmental partners within the Directorate of Youth and Sport. The role of this joint council is to develop a common position on the main aspects of the youth sector in the Council of Europe, namely priorities and objectives, as well as on the budget.

4. The Programming Committee. This is another joint decision-making body consisting of eight members of the European Steering Committee for Youth and eight members of the Advisory Council. The role of this committee is to establish programmes in the area of youth work within the Council of Europe, especially the programmes of the European Youth Centres in Strasbourg and Budapest and of the European Youth Foundation.

---

*Reflection time*

*1. Do you know of any example of co-management systems functioning at a local or organisational level? Where is it? How does it function?*

*2. What benefits of the co-management system can you think of?*

*3. In your opinion, what are the limitations of the co-management system?*

---

### *Co-management at a local level*

The revised charter states that "local and regional authorities should develop the Council of Europe co-management principle and system of decision-making in partnership with young people and youth organisations in policy areas relevant to young people."[43] This is considered a very special form of co-operation because all parties, both adults and young people, are on the same level and hold the same power to make decisions. It may, in some communities, be difficult for young people to be seen as equal partners with adults and to share power with them. The experience of various organisations shows, however, that "this concept opens the door to amazing new opportunities, ideas and challenges for young people and elders to stretch their creativity and commitment. It reduces prejudice, enhances clarity and simplicity of communication, which makes it valid and useful in any sector of daily life – family, school and business".[44]

Setting up a co-management system at a local level can be done in a number of ways and there is no universal recipe that applies equally to all. It is possible, however, to present a general framework that can guide the whole process, and this is presented below.

---

43. Ibid., II.7.53.ii.
44. "Co-management. A practical guide. Seeking excellence in youth participation at a local level", Peace Child International, 2006, p. 9. Available at: http://co-management.info.

*Step 1 – Preparation*

Good preparation can substantially contribute to the success of an initiative, and it is therefore important to ensure that enough time and attention is given to this stage of the process. Before talking to potential partners about establishing a co-management system, one needs to make sure that the potential partner:

- understands what co-management is. Studying publications about this form of co-operation, making contact with people who already have experience in this area and listening to their advice, can all be helpful;
- is clear about what he/she wants to achieve (what area of co-management and to what extent?);
- knows of institutions or communities where this system already operates. One can often learn from the experience of others! A good idea might be to establish personal contact with a representative of such an institution's or community's co-management system so that you can address questions directly to that person;
- is able to explain co-management to interested parties in a way they can understand. The concept of co-management can be quite new for some people and they may have doubts and reservations (especially those who would be sharing power with another party). One therefore needs to be prepared to discuss what co-management means in general, how it works in the area of youth work, what the experience of other institutions or communities is, what the benefits are and what challenges there might be, etc.;
- has some material ready. People might need some time to think about what they hear and they might want to read a bit more about it, so it would be helpful to provide them with relevant materials.

*Step 2 – Finding allies*

As a lot of support will be needed in the following stages, one should look for allies who would be interested in helping and joining the initiative. If one represents local youth or a youth organisation, it can be helpful to find like-minded people or organisations. If one represents local authorities, one can look for other officers who could provide support, or contact institutions working with youth in the area (such as schools, youth centres, etc.). Such allies can provide not only moral support, but they can also take over some tasks, help to generate better ideas and contribute resources, etc.

*Step 3 – Approaching a potential co-management partner*

This is a very important moment in the whole process as at this point the partnership is initiated between the parties who will be sharing the decision-making power and responsibilities. If the other party does not agree to participate in establishing the co-management system then the whole process will be blocked. Approaching the co-management partner is often a long process and one can expect a number of meetings and negotiations. Some tips:

- make a plan on how to approach your potential co-management partner. Decide how you want to do this, when, where and with whom, etc. Divide the roles and tasks between your allies;
- try to identify the fears and doubts your potential co-management partner may have in relation to your proposal. Think of ways of addressing these doubts;
- be ready to negotiate and to compromise. Your partner might be interested in creating a co-management system, but only to a limited extent (for example, only in the area of health care for young people in your local community). Starting on a small scale is a good way to initiate the whole co-management process and to learn how it works. When more experience has been gained, the co-management can be extended to other areas too;

- do not take no for an answer. Keep on trying (within reasonable limits, of course);
- be patient. The whole process can take some time, as changing people's attitudes does not happen during just one meeting.

### *Step 4 – Defining aims, areas of responsibility and ways of working*

When a partnership has been created to establish the co-management system, the hard work of working out the details of co-operation and the principles of the partnership can begin. All parties should be involved in discussions and in taking decisions, as at this stage a contract of sorts is created between the partners and guidelines for future work are set up. The following questions need to be answered:

- Who will be involved in the co-management system?
- Will there be any bodies or formal structures within the system? If so, which ones?
- How will the members of both parties be selected? How can it be ensured that local population is represented? How inclusive will the membership be?
- What role will the co-management system play? What areas will be involved and what will be the scope of decisions?
- What will be the rights and responsibilities of the parties?
- What working methods (or procedures, although young people are often not very motivated by procedures) will be used?
- What will be the basic principles of co-operation?
- How will the system be evaluated? How often? By whom?

### *Step 5 – Assessing the resources needed*

Having established the basis for co-operation in Step 4, the parties can now assess what they need in terms of preliminary plans and agreements. In considering what resources will be needed, one thinks immediately of finance, which, although very important, is not the only resource required. At this stage, it is also necessary to find out:

- How much time will the parties need to dedicate to the co-management system?
- What venue can be used for meetings? Is it youth-friendly? Is it accessible?
- Who can provide technical and secretarial support?
- What competencies and skills are needed for the efficient functioning of the co-management system (what knowledge do young people and local authorities representatives need to and what skills will need to be developed)?
- How can these needs be satisfied?

### *Step 6 – Planning the introductory phase*

At this stage the parties are ready to start planning the first phase of their work. The introduction of a co-management system can take some time, especially if local regulations need to be amended so that the co-management system can be officially recognised, or if technical arrangements have to be made or new documents produced, etc. The members of the co-management system bodies also need an introduction to the system or perhaps even some training before the system can work smoothly.

*Step 7 – Launching the establishment of the co-management system*

A co-management system serves the interests of the local community, and so the local community and especially the young people living there should be aware of its existence. Some communities choose to launch their co-management systems by means of a special celebration so that the whole community becomes aware of and can be proud of it.

*Next steps ...*

A co-management system is intended to be a long-term initiative and so the work and activities need to be planned on a regular basis. This might be every few months, every year or every two years, depending on the situation. It is crucial, however, that plans focus not only on dealing with local issues and decisions, but also on a regular evaluation of how the system is operating, so that its different aspects can be constantly improved.

> **Reflection time**
>
> 1. How realistic would it be to introduce the co-management system in your local community? Why do you think so?
> 2. Who, in your local context, would be interested in establishing the co-management system? What do you think would motivate them to do so?
> 3. In what areas of daily life, policies or programmes involving young people in your local context would the introduction of a co-management system be most relevant? Why do you think so?

The introduction of a co-management system can start on a small scale. In some contexts, for example, it is not realistic to expect that decisions concerning local budgets or other crucial issues will be made by or shared with young people. However, this should not be a reason for not introducing a co-management system at all. Small-scale systems such as the management of youth centres or local programmes for young people can work very well. Starting small is, in many cases, a good idea.

## 6.5. Other forms of co-operation in the area of decision making

Consultations, the creation of committees of representatives and the introduction of co-management systems are just a few examples of possible forms of co-operation between local actors in order to promote youth participation. Other forms of partnership-building exist, however, and communities should be able to find at least one that would be relevant for them. Examples of such forms of co-operation are given below.

*Common projects and initiatives*

Local authorities sometimes invite non-governmental organisations specialising in specific areas or topics to join initiatives and projects. In such cases, local authorities retain control of the whole initiative, but they establish a partnership with a local organisation in order to obtain expert advice or to use existing know-how, experience and infrastructure. In this way, local expertise can be used to address local problems.

*Delegating statutory tasks*

In some countries, local authorities have the freedom to delegate some of their statutory tasks to non-governmental organisations. On the basis of special agreements outlining the rights and responsibilities of both parties, organisations take over the implementation of local policies, such as environmental policy, policy on access to culture, etc., or take over the running of programmes, such as shelter services for homeless youth or feeding programmes. Sometimes these policies and programmes are directly related to youth issues and directly affect the lives of local young people. In such cases, a partnership between local authorities and youth organisations can be created through which organisations gain the support they need in order to improve the lives of young people in the community.

### Structural funding

Local budgets can secure funds for the so-called "structural funding" of youth organisations. This type of financial support does not cover the cost of projects and actions, but instead covers costs related to the everyday running of the organisation, employment costs or administration costs, for example. Structural funding can be very important for youth organisations with little experience in fund-raising, but also for informal youth groups or organisations that are run without permanent staff responsible for fund-raising.

### Grant system

Organisations can receive financial support from local authorities for activities and programmes run by them. These activities are planned and implemented independently from the local authorities, although the funds usually go to those activities that fit local priorities. There is an ongoing debate as to what extent these programmes and activities can be said to be really independent if support is granted only to those activities fitting the political agenda of a local authority.

### Guarantor

The revised charter mentions a special type of support available for organisations involved in youth participation – the appointment of a guarantor.[45] The guarantor can be either a person or a group who is independent from both political and youth participation structures. The main role of the guarantor is to act as an interface or channel of communication between young people and local authorities' representatives in cases of tension between the two parties.

### Other forms of co-operation

- exchange of information (about initiatives, plans, developments, etc.);
- creating joint advisory teams of governmental and non-governmental bodies working on different topics;
- inviting the representatives of the other party to open meetings, debates, etc.

---

*Reflection time*
1. Which forms of co-operation between local authorities, youth organisations and young people function in your local community or region?
2. How is information about this co-operation disseminated?
3. Who are the parties involved in this co-operation? What is your relationship to these parties?
4. Is your organisation/institution interested in co-operating at a local level with other partners?
5. Why?

---

45. III.1.70.

# CHAPTER 7
## The Charter and local youth policies

### 7.1. Introduction to local youth policy

"Public policy seeks to achieve goals that are considered to be in the best interests of all the members of the society."[46] Examples of this are safety, good quality health and social care, access to education, access to employment, etc. But not all public policies are relevant for all members of society; some deal with issues that are crucial only for a specific group such as young people, for example because the well-being of the young contributes to the well-being of the whole population. In this chapter, public policies related to young people and their needs and aspirations are referred to as "youth policies".[47]

The development of an effective youth policy has become an important goal for a growing number of countries in Europe and throughout the world. The Council of Europe supports these efforts by providing guidelines and legal instruments that help create or improve youth policies at local, national and European levels. Approaches to youth policy differ among member states. In some countries, it is considered an important area of work and the appropriate resources are provided and access to information, power and decision making is granted. In others, youth policy may constitute an element of other policy areas, such as education policy, sport, culture, tourism, etc. Different policy implementation methods also exist – the centralised method, where decisions and actions are co-ordinated from one central point (for example, a ministry or other agency responsible for youth affairs) – or the decentralised method, where decision-making power and resources are delegated to other levels, including regions and local communities.

> **Reflection time**
>
> 1. Are youth issues a priority for the government of your country? Why do you think so?
> 2. How does the national youth policy in your country operate? What are the aims and priority areas?
> 3. To what extent is national youth policy in your country decentralised?
> 4. Do you think that your youth policy has an "inclusive approach" to young people (meaning it takes all young people into account)?

---

46. Torjman, S., *What is policy?* Caledon Institute of Social Policy, 2005, p. 4.
47. This is, however, not a definition of youth policy. There is no consensus regarding the meaning of the term "youth policy".

This manual focuses mainly on youth policy at a local level. The revised charter says that young people are citizens in the municipalities and regions where they live,[48] and that, as a result, a youth policy should exist and be implemented at local level, so that the needs and aspirations of youth can be satisfied in the best possible way.

Well-functioning youth policy at the local level can generate a number of positive results, including, for example:

- identifying the most important needs of local young people;
- meeting these needs in an efficient way;
- improving the situation of young people;
- ensuring that youth issues are also addressed by other sectoral policies;
- creating a basis for the achievement of common goals through actors involved in working with and for youth;
- co-ordinating and channelling different initiatives and actions at a local level;
- providing a clear distribution of resources to satisfy the needs of local young people and entities working for the benefit of youth;
- recognising the contribution of young people to development of the local community;
- stimulating young people to play an active role in dealing with issues affecting their lives;
- providing a framework to plan the future of local youth;
- strengthening inter-generational dialogue and co-operation at a local level.

The above results can be achieved only if the development and implementation of the local youth policy is based on the following principles:

1. The policy has clearly defined goals and ways of achieving these goals. All the actors involved, as well as the local community as a whole, need to know precisely what should be achieved and how to get there.

2. The highest political level of a community or region is seriously committed to dealing with youth issues. This commitment means, in practice, that youth issues become one of the local priorities and that they get enough attention.

3. The resources necessary for the planning, implementation and evaluation of the local youth policy are available. Even the best plans and strategies will be inefficient if they are not backed up by the appropriate finance, time and know-how.

4. Young people play an active role in the planning, implementation and evaluation of local youth policy (at all stages). If youth policy is planned *for* young people but *without* them (a top-down approach), there is a risk that the policy will reflect the real needs of young people only to a limited extent. The young might feel no "ownership" of such a policy and so not be motivated to get involved in any aspect of it.

5. All the main actors working for and/or with youth are involved in the entire process. Each of them has his/her unique knowledge, experience, access to resources, position within the local context and role to play, and these assets can contribute to the creation and development of a relevant and good quality youth policy.

---

48. The revised European Charter on the Participation of Young People in Local and Regional Life. Introduction.

6. There is a strong partnership between the actors so that they can learn from each other and provide the necessary support.

7. Youth policy is cross-sectoral. This means that it deals with issues related to different areas, such as education, sport, culture, media, employment, housing, etc., because young people's lives encompass a wide variety of different areas.

8. Youth policy should be based on research. There are different ways of conducting research: from very complex methodologies and analysis to simple data collection. The research method should be chosen according to need and the resources available, but it should be ensured that the policy is not based on somebody's assumptions, but on the evidence and solid analysis of the local situation.

> *Reflection time*
>
> 1. Which of the above principles do you consider necessary for effective youth policy at a local level?
> 2. Which of these principles can bring an added value but are not strictly necessary for the effectiveness of local youth policy? Why?

Different generic approaches to youth policy can also be adapted to a local context. One such approach[49] is called the "fire brigade approach". It can be observed when local authorities react only to specific problems relating to young people. These problems are not seen as a part of a complex issue, but as isolated events that need to be solved as soon as possible (like small fires that need to be extinguished immediately). Once the situation has been dealt with, the issue is forgotten and the next problem is addressed. At present there is, however, a shift towards a different approach that places young people in the centre and treats them as a resource rather than a problem. When local authorities follow this philosophy, they try to ensure that young people have opportunities to develop their intellectual, social, artistic and physical potential, and that they can contribute their talents to the well-being of the whole community. It is believed that focusing on developing their strengths empowers young people to build better lives and prevents them from becoming involved in criminal activities or other destructive behaviour. Finally, there is an approach called "management by objectives".[50] It looks at local youth policy in terms of specific goals that need to be achieved and the implementation of these goals is carefully planned, carried out and evaluated. This approach focuses on introducing concrete changes and on checking the efficiency of the whole process.

> *Reflection time*
>
> 1. What advantages and disadvantages of these three approaches can you see in your local context?
> 2. Which (if any) of the above approaches to local youth policy is used in your community or region? How can you recognise it/them?

---

49. The approaches presented in this paragraph are quoted from Lauritzen, P., "Essentials of a youth policy in the Council of Europe", unpublished paper, p. 4.
50. For more information about managing by objectives, see Siurala, L., *European framework of youth policy*, Budapest, 2004.

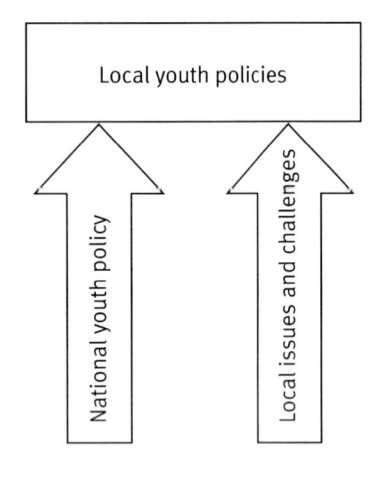

*Components of a local youth policy*

Local youth policy should consist of two main pillars. It should implement the relevant provisions of the national youth policy and should address the challenges of the specific community. As already mentioned, in the framework of national youth policy some tasks or objectives can be delegated to other decision-making levels, and also to regions and communities. It is therefore essential that the provisions of the national youth policy are known and implemented at local level. Sometimes the information flow between different decision-making levels needs to be improved, and it is the responsibility of local authorities to get information about a national youth policy and to look for ways of implementing it in their community or region. Youth policies can be formulated in a variety of ways. In some countries there are very few comprehensive documents addressing the most important aspects of young people's lives. In others, youth policy can exist as a number of fragmented regulations and legal provisions spread across various domains (separate laws related to young people within a national policy on employment, for example, or regulations within a policy on combating crime, etc.). Even in these cases, ministries or other central institutions responsible for youth should be able to provide details of the national youth policy, as well as information on what can and should be done at a local level.

## 7.2. The revised charter and local youth policy

The revised charter contains a number of recommendations for sectoral policies at a local and regional level. It is, however, important to remember that these recommendations relate mainly to different aspects of youth participation and leave aside a whole range of other issues that are important to young people in a local community. In spite of these limitations, the charter can be used as a useful tool to create a local youth policy. An explanation of how this can be done is given below.

### *Embracing the values promoted in the charter*

Youth policies are based on values and also promote them. "It's not hard to make decisions when you know what your values are."[51] For that reason, actors need to decide what values are important to them when creating local youth policy and how these values can translate into specific objectives and actions. The main values stressed in the charter are:

– *participation:* young people have a right to be involved in decisions affecting their lives and therefore have the right to be involved in the development and implementation of local youth policies;

– *freedom to chose to participate or not to participate:* young people should have the chance to participate, but they may also choose not to participate if they so wish;

– *non-discrimination:* young people are a diverse group but each individual should have the chance to play an active role in his/her local context, regardless of their background, education, financial status, disability, minority status, etc.;

---

51. Disney, R., an American film writer and nephew of Walt Disney.

- *multiculturalism:* diverse needs, customs, cultures and lifestyles should be respected;
- *having rights:* young people are citizens and members of the local community just as other people are. They should therefore have similar or equivalent rights (appropriate to their age and related to the obligations they have as community members);
- *respect:* young people should be treated with dignity and their views should be respected (but to respect somebody's view does not necessarily mean to agree);
- *partnership:* young people should be treated as partners in a decision-making process, not as a client waiting to be served;
- *responsibility:* young people, like any member of society, should be responsible for their actions;
- *empowerment:* young people have different talents and strengths that they can use to address their problems and challenges, but sometimes they need empowerment and support in order that they can develop and use these talents in the most efficient ways;
- *support:* young people have limited power and limited resources. They need support in order to play an active role in their community.

### *Using the examples of sectoral policies*

The charter contains a review of areas that play an important role in lives of young people at a local level. This review can help to structure the process of assessing the needs of young people in a community or region or can be used as a template to design local policies (although this template should be complemented by elements relevant to the specific circumstances). The charter also explains why specific areas should be addressed by local youth policies.

| Sectoral policy | Reasons for implementing this policy at a local level |
|---|---|
| A policy for sport, leisure and associative life | - activities are one of the pillars of social cohesion in the municipality or region;<br>- ideal channel for youth participation;<br>- ideal channel for the implementation of youth policies in the fields of sport, culture, crafts and trades, artistic and other forms of creation and expression, as well as in the field of social action. |
| A policy to promote youth employment and to combat unemployment | - the economic and social conditions experienced by young people influence their motivation and ability to participate;<br>- unemployment and poverty make it very difficult to be an active citizen;<br>- unemployed youth are likely to be among the most excluded in a society. |

| | |
|---|---|
| A policy on urban environment and habitat, housing and transport | – a more integrated and less fragmented living environment is conducive to social interaction and the development of high-quality public space;<br>– a more harmonious environment is conducive to personal self-fulfilment and development of solidarity between generations;<br>– mobility of young people is indispensable for participation in social life and for being full citizens;<br>– in rural areas, mobility and transport are fundamental necessities for a good quality of life and not just necessary to facilitate participation;<br>– a lack of transportation leads to exclusion. |
| An education and training policy promoting youth participation | – schools are places where young people's views and perspectives on life are shaped;<br>– schools are often the first places where students experience democracy in action and can practice participation. |
| A health policy | – young people are threatened by tobacco, alcohol and drug abuse;<br>– there is an observed increase in sexually transmitted diseases that results in moral judgments, leading to isolation. |
| A gender equality policy | – young men and women have difficulty in obtaining positions of responsibility within professional life, associations, politics and local and regional authorities;<br>– at local level, inequalities exist between young men and women. |
| A specific policy for rural regions | – young people from rural areas have different needs than their counterparts living in towns or cities regarding education, employment, housing, transportation, etc…;<br>– young people in rural areas experience a lower level of social services provision than those living in urban areas ;<br>– youth and community organisations stimulate social and cultural life in rural areas and can be an important social outlet for young people;<br>– youth and community organisations encourage participation of local youth;<br>– youth and community organisations improve the quality of life and combat problems of rural isolation. |
| A policy on access to culture | – art and culture are part of past, present and future personal and collective heritage and they are a reflection of each society;<br>– young people play a role in these cultural developments through their practice of culture and their capacity for initiative, exploration and innovation. |

| | |
|---|---|
| A policy for sustainable development and for the environment | – young people and other members of society are faced with deterioration of the environment;<br>– environmental problems are of primary concern to young people who will be obliged, in the future, to cope with the consequences of past mistakes. |
| A policy to combat violence and crime | – young people are often victims of crime, violence, sexual exploitation, abuse or other forms of mistreatment;<br>– there are different forms of violence in schools;<br>– adequate responses to the crime and violence in contemporary society are missing. |
| An anti-discrimination policy | – there is discrimination against minorities, including young members of minority groups;<br>– there is discrimination against people with disabilities and other groups;<br>– in some communities, equal access to public places, vocational training, schooling, housing, cultural activities and to other areas of life is not guaranteed. |
| A policy on sexuality | – during the transition from childhood dependence to autonomous adult life, young people might be faced with issues connected to their personal relationships;<br>– there is persistent ignorance surrounding issues of sexual health;<br>– there is mistrust of official attitudes concerning the risks of certain sexual behaviour;<br>– the emergence and exercise of young people's sexuality is not always easy. |
| A policy of access to rights and law | – societies are based on rules that must be respected by all in order to live harmoniously together;<br>– in democratic societies, the rules are discussed and adopted by the elected representatives of citizens;<br>– legal texts and rules increase in number and it gets more and more difficult for an individual to know about and to apply them;<br>– the increasing number of rules and laws creates disparities between citizens (as some are aware of their rights and obligations and others are not). |

The above list of reasons for introducing youth policy in some specific areas of public life is not exhaustive and is meant as a sample and a starting point for further analysis. The main role of the charter is to promote youth participation in general and as a result it does not deal with a number of issues (inter-generational relations, conflict prevention, etc.) and deals with other issues only to a limited extent. It therefore falls to local actors involved in developing youth policy to identify areas that are still missing from the charter.

> *Reflection time*
>
> 1. What values promoted in the charter would you consider the most important in your local community? Why?
> 2. Which of the sectoral policies presented above are already a part of local youth policies in your communities?
> 3. What other sectoral policies not present in the charter does your local youth policy contain?
> 4. What sectoral policies are still missing from your local context?

## 7.3. Formulation process of a local youth policy

The formulation of a local youth policy is a complex procedure and it requires the involvement of various actors. Local authorities, as the main body dealing with local policies, have substantial expertise and experience in this field and therefore they should play an active role in the whole process of local youth policy development. This process will differ from country to country due to existing traditions, norms, procedures and laws, and presenting one universal model for all the different situations in Europe is not possible. There are, however, a number of suggestions that can be helpful when working on local youth policy.

### *Building up partnerships*

An efficient youth policy at local level needs the involvement of various actors: local authorities, young people, local organisations and institutions. Some communities use a top-down approach, which means that local authorities decide on the policy and then implement it on their own or try to find partners who will implement it. This, however, is not a very participatory approach, and it is strongly recommended that different actors are involved in the whole process from a very early stage.

### *Being clear why a local youth policy is needed at a local level*

Developing local youth policies is currently in fashion and a growing number of communities have shown interest in dealing with youth issues in a more coherent and efficient way. Having a good youth policy at local level can bring real benefits and changes, so once the process of creating such policy has been initiated, it is important to identify what concrete changes and improvements should be made.

### *Collecting information about the national and regional youth policy*

As already discussed, a local youth policy should be built on two pillars, one of them being the national youth policy. When the national policy delegates some objectives or actions to other levels, it is necessary to find out exactly what these delegated responsibilities are, and whether any guidelines are provided to help implement them, so that their implementation can be planned in the framework of local youth policy. A national policy should also address the whole range of issues relevant at local level, so local policy makers are given guidance and inspiration for their work.

### *Analysing the situation of young people in the local community – Identifying needs*

Another pillar of local youth policy focuses on issues especially important for a local community. These issues might not be addressed by a national youth policy, which has a limited scope and focuses only on a number of priority areas relevant to all the young people living in a country. It is therefore essential to analyse the situation of young people in a local community and to decide which additional areas, problems and challenges should be addressed by a local youth policy. In such a way, it can be ensured that local youth policy reflects the needs and aspirations of young people and that it is not just part of the political agenda of local decision makers.

### *Identifying and evaluating various youth-related programmes and actions at a local level*

Even if there is no official local youth policy, there are probably various projects, events and initiatives, either formal or informal, taking place in the community. They have a real potential to bring positive changes in young people's lives and can contribute to the implementation of local youth policy, and so actors involved in policy creation need to know exactly what is going on and which organisations, institutions or groups are involved.

### *Setting priorities*

Young people are a diverse group and this means they have different needs and expectations. It might be impossible to meet all of these in the framework of a local youth policy using the available resources and therefore priorities need to be set. Deciding on priorities is a very important and sometimes difficult step, as one needs to assess the value of the issues at hand. Priorities should not be chosen on the basis of the personal or organisational preferences of the parties involved, but on a solid analysis of the situation.

### *Defining vision/aims/objectives/strategy/plan of action/evaluation*

There are different formulas that can be used to develop local policies; some communities start by describing a vision, others prefer to focus on formulating aims and objectives. There is no one right or wrong way to do this. Local policy makers should just be clear about what they want to achieve, in what time frame, with what resources, how they plan to do it and how they want to evaluate the whole process. Youth policy, like any other initiative, should be evaluated on a regular basis, and the evaluation needs to be planned together with all the other elements of the policy.

### *Consultations about the policy proposal*

All parties involved in the process of creating a local youth policy and interested in youth issues at a local level need to be given a chance to comment and express their opinions about the final policy proposal. This can be done through a round of consultations or through meetings, workshops, surveys, etc.

### *Adopting the policy*

A youth policy can have a different type of status at the local level. It might remain at the level of an agreement between different partners, but it might also be officially recognised by local authorities and adopted as one area of local public policy. In the latter case, the local authorities would get the political responsibility for implementing this policy and would be accountable to the whole community for the results.

*Dissemination*

The information about a local youth policy should be disseminated in the local community or region so that those who are interested in it can get involved. Special attention should be given to informing young people about such a policy, as they will be the main beneficiaries of it.

*Participatory monitoring of the policy implementation*

There should be systematic control or examination of different aspects of the policy implementation (monitoring) in order to assess the progress being made in relation to specific objectives. Monitoring helps not only to check how efficiently the resources are being used, but also helps to identify successes and problems at an early stage. It also ensures that a policy can be adapted in the event of changes in the situation in a community or society. Participatory monitoring means that the monitoring involves different local actors and young people in particular.

---

*Reflection time*

1. How would you describe the local youth policy in your community or region? What are its priorities?
2. To which extent does this policy reflect your country's national youth policy?
3. Who was involved in shaping the local policy?
4. Who is involved in implementing it?
5. How is the youth policy monitored?

---

## 7.4. Advocacy – Networking for policy change

Although youth policy in general is becoming an important issue at a local level, in some communities the priorities lie elsewhere. Different organisations, institutions and individuals are trying to ensure that youth issues get enough attention by becoming involved in advocacy, which can be defined as a set of targeted actions directed at decision makers in support of a specific policy issue,[52] and also by creating advocacy networks. Advocacy aims at influencing different aspects of youth policy, such as the public perception of certain issues or the attitudes of policy makers. It can also aim at supporting specific solutions or even stopping certain proposals. Advocacy can be used at various levels – institutional, local, regional, national and international.

Advocacy is based on networking – creating and maintaining contacts with those who support the same aims and who agree to work on achieving common goals. In fact, almost everybody is a part of some network or another – at work, at school, in social life or sports activities – in general people know quite a lot about this form of co-operation and use it skilfully. Advocacy networks need to be organised in such a way that time, motivation and other resources are used in the most efficient way in order to achieve the aims.

In some cases, an advocacy network evolves into a coalition (a kind of union) and this is invaluable because it brings people and resources from all sectors of the community together and provides a visible sign of community support.[53] Working as part of a coalition helps to spread responsibilities and creates the space to engage in group

---

52. *Networking for policy change. An advocacy training manual*, The Policy Project, 1999, p. I-1.
53. "Advocacy kit", Advocates for Youth Washington, available at: www.advocatesforyouth.org/publications/advocacykit.pdf.

problem-solving. It is, however, a rather close form of co-operation, and sometimes the interests of coalition members differ, causing further difficulties.

When setting up a network, one needs to reflect on the following questions:

- What is the purpose of the network?
- What skills, expertise and resources will be needed to achieve this purpose?
- Who can bring these skills, expertise and resources to the network? Which individuals, organisations and institutions should be a part of this network?
- What kind of commitment will be necessary from the network members?
- How can potential members be encouraged to join the network?
- Who should do this?
- When should the first meeting take place?
- What should be on the agenda?
- What should be the structure?
- How should decisions be made?
- What form should the leadership take?
- How should the co-operation operate?
- How should the information flow operate?
- How should potential conflicts be dealt with?
- How should a plan of action be developed?
- How can the necessary resources be obtained?
- How should the plan of action be monitored and evaluated?
- What kind of support is needed for the network to function (for example, secretarial support)? How can it be obtained?

Advocacy work is based, to a large extent, on effective communication, and for this reason the advocacy network members should possess or develop the skills that ensure the best possible communication. This is crucial, not only for contacts with policy makers, but also for maintaining good working relations within the network. The skills needed relate to formulating opinions, expressing thoughts and feelings, transmitting messages, giving good quality presentations, and reading non-verbal signals, as well as active listening and encouraging other speakers to talk.

Understanding how policy processes function at a local level is essential for the success of the advocacy team. The members need to know how policies are created (procedures, formal rules and conditions), who is involved and in what capacity, what the power of specific actors is, etc. When all this information has been collected, it is possible to identify realistic objectives and the most efficient ways of approaching policy makers in order to achieve these objectives. Network members should be able to demonstrate this knowledge, as many policy makers perceive non-governmental organisations, for example, as lacking the knowledge and experience necessary for involvement in the policy formulation process. Such attitudes block advocacy efforts and can lead to a refusal to co-operate.

> *Reflection time*
>
> 1. *How would you evaluate your communication skills? What are your strengths and weaknesses?*
> 2. *How are policies created in your country?*
> 3. *How are policies created in your region or local community?*
> 4. *Have you ever been involved in a policy formulation or implementation process? In what capacity?*

### *Steps in the advocacy process*[54]

**Step 1 – Defining the issue**

The network needs to agree on what issue to support in order to promote a policy change. This issue should be in line with the mission of the network and should fulfil previously agreed criteria.

**Step 2 – Setting aims and objectives**

The network needs to briefly define what it wants to achieve in the longer term (aims) and then to plan a set of specific, measurable and short-term achievements that will contribute to the aims.

**Step 3 – Identifying the target audience**

The primary target audience is the policy makers who have the power to introduce a new policy or a policy change. The secondary target audience is all those who have access to and can influence the primary target audience, such as other policy makers, politicians, local authority employees, the media, local leaders, etc. The network needs to identify who these individuals or groups are, what power they have and what their attitudes are towards the proposed policy change (namely, whether they are for it, against it or neutral).

**Step 4 – Building support**

Network members should look for support from among those organisations, institutions, networks, civic groups, coalitions, activists or individuals who are interested in the issue concerned and who would be willing to help them achieve their goals. The success of the initiative depends to a large extent on the support base, so there should be enough time and resources planned for this task.

**Step 5 – Developing the message**

Advocacy messages should be formulated in such a way that the target audience can be persuaded to offer its support to the network proposal. The message should therefore be tailored to fit the profile of the target audience and should clearly express what is expected.

**Step 6 – Setting channels for communication**

Your target audience will determine the choice of communication channels. Different ways of passing on the advocacy message need to be used when trying to reach decision makers, when educating the local community or when looking for support from like-minded groups and individuals. At a local level, the communication channels can include press releases in local media, local debates, meetings with policy makers and fact sheets, etc.

---

54. Model presented in *Networking for policy change. An advocacy training manual*, The Policy Project, 1999, pp. III-7-III-9.

**Step 7 – Raising funds**

Advocacy initiatives need financial support to cover the costs of materials, travel (when attending meetings with decision makers, for example), meeting infrastructure (such as renting a meeting venue) and communication costs between the network members, etc. In order not to be reliant only on financial contributions from network members, the establishment of a fund-raising strategy early on in the advocacy process can also help generate external financial support.

**Step 8 – Developing an implementation plan**

The network needs to plan how the entire advocacy campaign should be run. The plan should include a list of all activities and tasks and should specify the responsibilities given to each person or group. It should also set a time frame for completion of all activities, and should list the resources needed, as well as explaining how these resources will be obtained.

## *Ongoing activities*

- collecting data is important at various stages of the whole advocacy campaign. It is helpful when identifying the main issues that need to be dealt with in developing appropriate objectives, with formulation of the advocacy message, when seeking support and also when influencing policy makers;
- monitoring and evaluation should also take place throughout the advocacy campaign. Both activities should be planned in advance so that progress and results can be assessed.

Advocacy is a very powerful method of achieving policy changes or initiating the development of new policies in different contexts and at various levels. Its potential, however, is not used sufficiently in local communities (especially in relation to youth issues) in spite of the fact that advocacy makes it much easier to establish personal contacts with local policy makers and to build direct relations with actors concerned. To a large extent, this happens because people who work for and with young people are convinced that advocacy work demands some special skills and competencies that they do not possess. And they forget that advocacy work is based mainly on the commitment and motivation of the parties concerned.

---

*Reflection time*

1. What policy changes (in the youth or any other field) could benefit from the advocacy process in your community or region?
2. Who would be interested in supporting such a policy change?
3. What target audience should be approached?
4. Which channels of communication would be the most efficient?

# CHAPTER 8
## Educational section

Undertaking participatory work and using the revised charter as a practical tool requires some degree of knowledge, skills and the right attitude regarding youth participation. As a result, all those interested in youth involvement at a local level might need specific training and support. These needs can be addressed in a variety of ways, one such way being by the provision of workshops that explore different dimensions of youth participation or that help participants to identify possible ways of using the revised charter in their own context. Information that helps the preparation of such workshops is available either on the Internet or directly from organisations working on education for participation.

In this chapter, we describe various educational activities that can be used as part of training related to youth participation in general, or to the charter, in particular. These activities have been either adopted from different educational sources or developed for the needs of this manual.

The methods presented are:

**Diamond of policies**
**Human sandwiches**
**Knives and forks**
**Ladder of participation**
**Meeting the mayor**
**Participation grid**
**Participation snowball**
**Participation timeline**
**Rights and participation**
**RMSOS charades**
**Role play on the charter**
**Statement exercise**

The triangle of co-operation
True or false?
What can you do for me?
Visit to Jeunessia
What happens if it doesn't happen?
Simulation exercise "Youth in action"

| Diamond of policies ||
|---|---|
| **Title** | Diamond of policies |
| **Theme** | Local policies enhancing youth participation |
| **Sample** | What's the most important? |
| **Group size** | Any |
| **Time** | 90 minutes |
| **Objectives** | − to introduce the content of the revised charter;<br>− to review local policies enhancing youth participation;<br>− to stimulate discussion about local youth policies in participants' contexts;<br>− to promote negotiation skills. |
| **Preparation** | To copy the sets of cards for each small group participating in the "Diamond of policies" activity. |
| **Materials** | One set of cards per small group. |
| **Instructions** | 1. Ask participants what they understand by the term "local policy".<br>2. Briefly introduce the different sectoral policies addressed in the revised charter.<br>3. Divide the participants into small groups of 4 people coming from the same region (either within a country or within Europe) and give a set of cards to each group.<br>4. Explain the procedure. Each group should briefly discuss the relevance of the policies mentioned on the cards to their own situations. Then they should negotiate which policies are the most relevant and least relevant for young people in their regions, and which are less relevant. The policy cards should be then arranged in a diamond pattern. The card with the most relevant policy should be put at the top of the diamond shape. Underneath this, two cards should be placed side by side and these should represent the next most relevant policies. The middle of the diamond should be made up of three cards representing moderately relevant policies. Underneath these, there should follow two cards showing less relevant policies and finally, at the bottom of the diamond, there should be one card, representing the policy that is least relevant to the participants' contexts.<br>5. Ask the groups to present their diamonds to the rest and to explain their choices. |

| | |
|---|---|
| **Debriefing and evaluation** | Ask participants the following questions: <br> 1. What does "relevant" mean to you? How did you define this word for the purpose of this exercise? <br> 2. Which policies are considered the most relevant for all the groups? Why? <br> 3. What are the differences between the diamonds? <br> 4. How do local policies influence participation of young people? <br> 5. Are you happy with the result of your work? Why? <br> 6. What was your influence on the whole negotiation process? <br> 7. What did you learn from this exercise? |
| **Variations** | 1. Instead of introducing the sectoral policies of the charter, the facilitator can ask the participants what local policies exist that are important for young people in their local communities or regions. <br> 2. If the participants are familiar with the charter, the facilitator can review what they remember that it says about sectoral policies. |
| **Attached documents** | Diamond of policies – Sample set of cards |

## DIAMOND OF POLICIES – Sample set of cards

| | |
|---|---|
| Policy for sport, leisure, associative life | Policy promoting youth employment |
| Specific policy for rural regions | Education policy promoting youth participation |
| Policy for sustainable development and for the environment | Anti-discrimination policy |
| Transport policy | Health policy |
| Policy for mobility and exchanges | |

| Human sandwiches ||
|---|---|
| **Title** | **Human sandwiches** <br> Source: *Training course on active youth participation*, EYC, Strasbourg, 2007. |
| **Theme** | Getting to know each other and exploring realities of youth participation |
| **Sample** | Me and my reality of youth participation |
| **Group size** | 12-35 |
| **Time** | 1 hour |
| **Objectives** | – to get to know each other; <br> – to share experience of youth participation realities related to participants' communities and organisations; <br> – to explore experiences of youth participation. |
| **Preparation** | Big room or space with indicated four thematic corners for sharing should be prepared. |
| **Materials** | A3 paper, markers or crayons, music |

| Instructions | **Individual preparation – 15 minutes** |
|---|---|
| | Participants receive two sheets of A3 paper and markers or crayons. |
| | On each of them they can draw or write about the following aspects of their life/experience: |
| |     – personal (family, studies, free time …); |
| |     – organisation/work; |
| |     – community/young people – characteristics; |
| |     – experiences of youth participation (action related). |
| | **Sharing – 40 minutes** |
| | Once the participants are ready they have to dress like "human sandwiches" between the two pieces of A3 paper (one paper in front, one paper on the back). |
| | Then they gather in the middle of a big room or space with the four thematic corners, which should be the same as these on their A3 papers. |
| | The corners are explained and participants are instructed that there will be four rounds and they have to pass through all the corners during the exercise. |
| | Some music is played and participants can mingle and look at each other's "sandwiches". |
| | When the facilitator stops the music the participants should choose one corner and share views on the topic indicated on the "sandwich" (for example, organisation/work). |
| | After 10 minutes the facilitator plays the music and the "human sandwiches" have to gather in the middle. When the music stops they choose a new corner. |
| | This is repeated four times. |
| **Debriefing and evaluation** | None |

| Knives and forks ||
|---|---|
| Title | **Knives and forks** |
| | Source: PLA Notes (2001), Issue 42, pp. 66-68, IIED London, Josh Levene |
| Theme | Principles of participation |
| Sample | To participate or not to participate? |
| Group size | 6-20 |

| Time | 60 minutes |
|---|---|
| **Objectives** | – to introduce the participants to some of the principles of participation;<br>– to explore how empowerment depends on transparency and sharing;<br>– to experience being in a situation where participation is a challenge. |
| **Preparation** | Find one person within the group of participants to share the secret rule of the game. |
| **Materials** | A knife and a fork<br>Flipchart, paper, pens |
| **Instructions** | 1. Participants sit in a circle.<br>2. Tell everyone that the rules of the game will be explained only once, so that they need to listen carefully.<br>3. Explain that you want everybody to concentrate on how they feel during the game.<br>4. The participants are required to pass on the knife and fork, either crossed or uncrossed, to the person sitting next to them. As they do so they should tell the whole group whether the knife and fork are "crossed" or "uncrossed". The facilitator will then tell them whether or not they are right.<br>5. Do not give any more instructions, even if there are more questions.<br>6. The facilitator starts the whole activity. The secret rule is that announcing "crossed" or "uncrossed" does not depend on the position of the knife and the fork, but on the position of the speaker's legs – whether they are crossed or not. The knife and fork can be positioned in any way a participant likes, but they will be correct only if their announcement matches the position of their legs.<br>7. After about 10 minutes, stop the game, as this is normally enough time for the participants to experience a whole range of emotions.<br>8. Ask those who have not discovered the secret rule how they are feeling. Write down their responses on a flipchart.<br>9. Ask those who have discovered the secret rule how they are feeling. Write down their answers.<br>10. Ask somebody from the group to explain the secret rule to the rest of the group.<br>11. Ask the participants who discovered the secret rule why they did not reveal it to the others (they very rarely do so). |

| | |
|---|---|
| **Debriefing and evaluation** | 1. Ask the participants what link they see between their experiences during this exercise (and the things they experienced during this exercise) and participation. Which aspects of participation have been tackled in this exercise?
2. Divide the participants so as to work in small discussion groups (two or four groups). Each of them should be focusing on the following sets of questions:

Set A

    a. When I am disempowered I feel …

    b. Towards those who disempower me I feel …

    c. Examples are …

    d. We are unable to participate when …

Set B

    e. When I am empowered I feel …

    f. Towards those who empower me I feel …

    g. Examples are …

    h. We are able to participate when …

3. If there are more than two groups, ask the groups working on Set A to get together and the groups working on Set B to get together. They should share ideas and record them on a flipchart.
4. Ask the groups to present the results of their work.
5. Initiate a plenary discussion on the advantages of participation and disadvantages of non-participation. |
| **Tips for the facilitator** | − the one person with whom you share the secret rule before the game begins should be sitting opposite you in the circle, so that both of you can check if participants' legs are crossed or not.
− be sensitive when using this exercise as people can become very defensive and emotional. |
| **Variations** | − the debriefing discussion can focus more on the role of sharing information, facts and rules in enabling people to participate.
− this exercise can be used to introduce the charter approach to youth participation based on right, means, space, opportunity and support (RMSOS). |

| Ladder of participation ||
|---|---|
| Title | **The ladder of participation**<br>Source: Training Course on the Development and Implementation of Participation Projects at Local and Regional Level, EYC, Strasbourg, 2005 |
| Theme | Implementing participatory projects |
| Sample | How "participatory" is your project? |
| Group size | Any |
| Time | 90 minutes |
| Objectives | – to reflect on possible degrees of youth participation in the framework of a project;<br>– to introduce the concept of the ladder of participation;<br>– to provide a framework to assess the degree of young people's participation in projects;<br>– to collect ideas for criteria of participatory projects. |
| Preparation | A big picture of Roger Hart's ladder of participation should be drawn on paper (or made out of tape on the floor). |
| Materials | None |
| Instructions | 1. Introduce the concept of degrees/levels of youth participation and the model of the ladder of participation.<br>2. Ask the participants to think about which rung of the ladder of participation best represents the degree of participation of young people in their project or community.<br>3. Ask the participants to stand by the relevant rung on the ladder.<br>4. Interview the participants: where does your project appear on the ladder of participation? How do you know this?<br>5. Invite the participants to brainstorm on possible ways of ensuring that young people can more fully participate in their project.<br>6. Individual reflection: which of the ideas generated during the brainstorming session can I use in my project? Why and how? |
| Debriefing and evaluation | Ask participants the following questions:<br>1. How useful do you find the model of the ladder of participation in your own work and in your own situation?<br>2. What are the limitations of this model? |

| Tips for the facilitator | Explain that the aim of this activity is not to reach the highest rung of the ladder and that the highest rungs do not necessarily mean the best rungs! You can also use rungs without numbers or a form other than a ladder (for example, a flower, see attached). |
|---|---|
| Variations | This activity can relate not only to youth projects, but also to youth involvement within different institutions or organisations. |
| Attached documents | A description of the concept of the ladder of participation (source: Chapter 1 of the manual) |

## THE LADDER OF PARTICIPATION – Explanation

Rung 8: Shared decision making
Rung 7: Young people led and initiated
Rung 6: Adult initiated, shared decision making
Rung 5: Young people consulted and informed
Rung 4: Young people assigned and informed
Rung 3: Young people tokenised
Rung 2: Young people as decoration
Rung 1: Young people manipulated

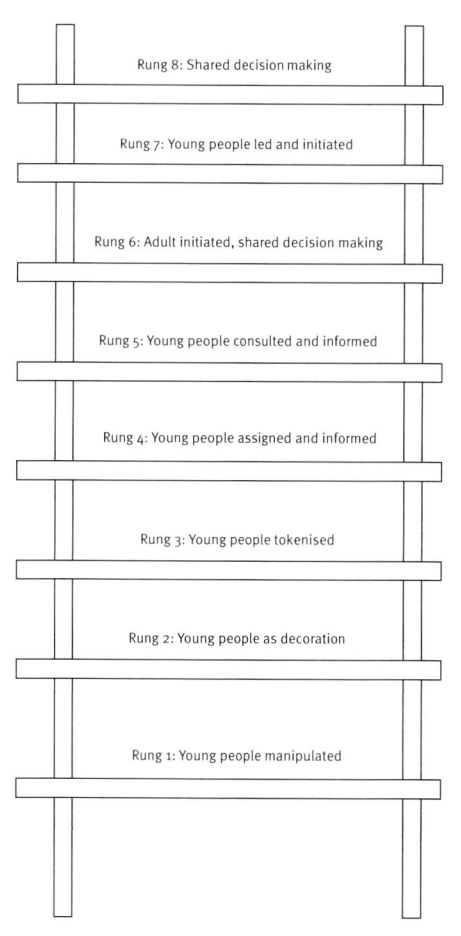

Adapted from: Hart, R., *Children's participation from tokenism to citizenship*, UNICEF Innocenti Research Centre, Florence 1992.

Rung 8: Shared decision making

Projects or ideas are initiated by young people, who invite the adults to take part in the decision-making process as partners.

Rung 7: Young people led and initiated

Projects or ideas are initiated and directed by young people; the adults might get invited to provide any necessary support, but a project can carry on without their intervention.

Rung 6: Adult initiated, shared decision making

Adults initiate projects but young people are invited to share the decision-making power and responsibilities as equal partners.

Rung 5: Young people consulted and informed

Projects are initiated and run by adults, but young people provide advice and suggestions and are informed how these suggestions contribute to the final decisions or results.

Rung 4: Young people assigned and informed

Projects are initiated and run by adults; young people are invited to take on some specific roles or tasks within the project, but they are aware of what influence they have in reality.

Rung 3: Young people tokenised (tokenism)

Young people are given some roles within projects but they have no real influence on any decisions. The illusion is created (either on purpose or unintentionally) that young people participate, when in fact they have no choice about what they do and how.

Rung 2: Young people as decoration

Young people are needed in the project to represent youth as an underprivileged group. They have no meaningful role (except from being present) and – as happens with any decorations – they are put in a visible position within a project or organisation, so that they can easily be seen by outsiders.

Rung 1: Young people manipulated

Young people are invited to take part in the project, but they have no real influence on decisions and their outcomes. In fact, their presence is used to achieve some other goal, such as winning a local election, creating a better impression of an institution or securing some extra funds from institutions that support youth participation.

## FLOWER OF PARTICIPATION – Explanation

*Source: CHOICE for Youth and Sexuality Foundation, the Netherlands, inspired by Roger Hart's ladder of participation*

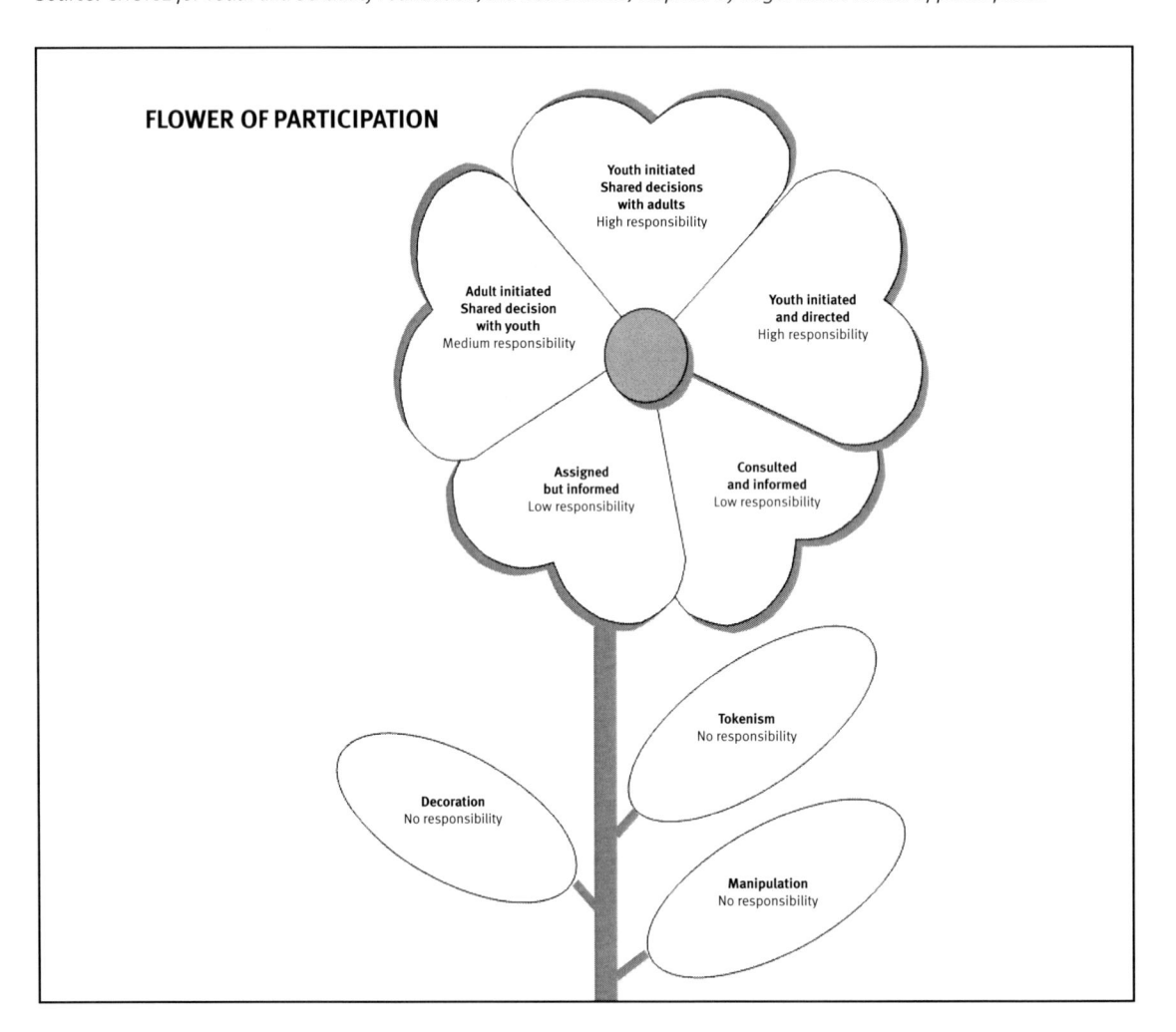

**FLOWER OF PARTICIPATION**

- Youth initiated, Shared decisions with adults — High responsibility
- Adult initiated, Shared decision with youth — Medium responsibility
- Youth initiated and directed — High responsibility
- Assigned but informed — Low responsibility
- Consulted and informed — Low responsibility
- Tokenism — No responsibility
- Decoration — No responsibility
- Manipulation — No responsibility

| \multicolumn{2}{|c|}{Meeting the mayor} |
|---|---|
| Title | **Meeting the mayor** <br> Source: *Training course on active youth participation*, EYC, Strasbourg, 2007. |
| Theme | Co-operation between NGOs and local authorities (LA) |
| Sample | Let's team up |
| Group size | 12-35 |
| Time | 120 minutes |
| Objectives | – to confront the participants with their own practices of youth participation; <br> – to open reflection on the communication and co-operation strategies between youth NGOs and local authorities; <br> – to identify aspects to improve. |
| Preparation | Copying and possibly adapting a case study; briefing the team from the local authority; setting the meeting place |
| Materials | Some clothing for the representatives of the local authorities (for example, ties, jacket etc.) |
| Instructions | 1. **Case study in working groups – 45 minutes** <br><br> Participants are divided into small groups. Each of the groups represents a youth community centre (NGO). All the groups receive the same case study and should prepare for a meeting with the local authorities. <br><br> The case study is written in the form of an invitation letter for a meeting of the team in order to prepare a consultative meeting with the mayor and other representatives of the local authorities. <br><br> A facilitator goes around the groups to make sure that the task is understood and to clarify any questions that participants might have. <br><br> If there are several groups the facilitator can act as co-ordinator of the umbrella youth NGO, which is organising the meeting with the mayor. <br><br> **Case study:** <br><br> "Invitation <br> From the co-ordinator (the facilitator) of "Just do it" – umbrella youth organisation <br> Dear team members, <br> We all work together in the youth community centre in a district of the city of Strasbourg. <br> For several months now, there are more and more signs, that show that young people are unhappy with their situation (living conditions, employment situation, etc.). <br> Recently, through isolated small events, some young people have started to express, in a violent way, their dissatisfaction (deterioration of a sports centre, supermarkets, etc.). <br> Two weeks ago a group of youngsters and some policemen were involved in a conflict, which resulted in a fight. As a result, a young person was badly injured and is in hospital, and two others have been arrested. |

Since then the situation is getting worse:

- some youngsters have started to burn cars in the district, and more and more cars are burned;
- such kinds of manifestation have started to happen in other districts of the city;
- every night there are confrontations with the police;
- other youngsters wanted to show that there are other ways of expression and started to organise peaceful manifestations, burning their ID cards as a symbol to show that even if legally they are equal citizens in reality they are not, believing that they do not have the same rights and opportunities.

For us at the youth community centre, it is time to react!

Therefore we will organize a meeting of our organisation in which we will work on two directions:

1. A short-term action plan: what to do concretely and how to try to avoid further incidents.

2. A mid-term action plan: in one year there are local elections, and we should use the opportunity to start to lobby the local authorities now, and make a strategic proposal including directions of work, educational approach, steps and concrete actions.

The above-mentioned events have started to happen in other districts of the city as well. The other branches of our organisation in these districts are also organising this meeting.

After our meeting, another meeting will be organised with representatives of the municipality of Strasbourg and other representatives from the youth structures from other districts to present our proposals/strategies.

Our task will be for two of our representatives to make a clear presentation of our strategy.

Many thanks for your co-operation and see you at the meeting.

The co-ordinator of "Just do it".

(Note: the case study/invitation should be adopted according to the objectives of the session and the activity.)

**Roles and guidelines for the briefing of the representatives of the local authority**

*Roles*

- mayor;
- political adviser in charge of internal and security affairs;
- deputy mayor in charge of youth affairs.

The roles can be played also by team members who are not in charge of introducing, facilitating or debriefing the exercise.

|  |  |
|---|---|
|  | **Guidelines for the briefing**<br>– the three representatives of the local authorities should have different approaches in their interventions. For example: mayor – searching for a quick and good solution for the whole city (considering arguments of his/her colleagues); political adviser – needs to insure the security of the citizens, is in favour of law and order, does not believe in a responsible youth; deputy mayor – responsible for youth and in contact with the youth NGOs, therefore in favour of a solution which includes and supports young people and youth NGOs also on a longer term basis.<br>– for its actual performance the actors are free to improvise according to their perceptions of a real-life meeting, however, they might need to sit together in advance in order to clarify their interventions.<br>– the mayor facilitates the meeting, as he/she is the host.<br><br>**2. Meeting between youth organisations and the local authorities – 30 minutes**<br><br>Each of the youth NGOs (working groups) sends two members from the organisation to the meeting with the mayor; the "co-ordinator" of "just do it" is unfortunately not available.<br><br>The mayor opens the meeting and announces the maximum duration of the meeting as 30 minutes).<br><br>The subject of the meeting is to discuss the proposals of the youth NGOs and to decide on possible action to remedy the current situation.<br><br>The rest of the participants are active observers of the meeting. They have the possibility to send notes through the facilitator (co-ordinator) to their colleagues, who are representing their NGO in the meeting.<br><br>**3. De-rolling**<br><br>Should be considered before the debriefing of the exercise. The facilitator can choose the method. |
| **Debriefing and evaluation** | **1. Feelings:**<br>– General? In the working groups on the case study? In the role play?<br><br>**2. Process:**<br>– Was it easy to prepare the strategies in the working groups? Why?<br><br>**3. Results:**<br>– What do you think about the results? Are the proposals relevant? What is missing? Did you identify any aspects that can be improved in your practice?<br><br>**4. Transfer to reality:**<br>– Is there any connection between the exercise and reality?<br>– What did you learn from this exercise? What can you use in your practice?<br>– Any comments or tips regarding co-operation with the local authorities? |

| Participation grid ||
|---|---|
| **Title** | **Participation grid**<br>Source: Clare Lardner, Clarity company,<br>www.clarity-scotland.pwp.blueyonder.co.uk |
| **Theme** | Power versus participation in a project |
| **Sample** | Who has the power? |
| **Group size** | Any |
| **Time** | 60 minutes |
| **Objectives** | – to understand the complexity of participation dimensions;<br>– to assess the degree of empowerment offered by different forms of participation or specific projects;<br>– to provide a concrete tool for comparing various forms of participation. |
| **Preparation** | A brief presentation of the "clarity model of participation" should be given on the basis of the grid handout. |
| **Materials** | Copies of the clarity model of participation grid handout |
| **Instructions** | 1. Ask the participants to think of a specific youth project they are involved in. Using the clarity model of participation, they should assess the degree to which adults and young people have power within this project.<br>2. Ask the participants to share the results of their work in groups of four.<br>3. Open the floor for any comments, remarks or questions.<br>4. Initiate a discussion on the theme: "How do the power relations within a project influence the participation of young people?" |
| **Debriefing and evaluation** | Ask participants the following questions:<br>1. Are you surprised by the results of your assessment? Why?<br>2. Did you learn anything new about your project? What?<br>3. How useful do you find this model in your youth work?<br>4. What do you think is needed in order to reach an "ideal" sharing of power between the actors? |
| **Attached documents** | Clarity model of participation handout |

## CLARITY MODEL OF PARTICIPATION

*Source: Clare Lardner, Clarity company, www.clarity-scotland.pwp.blueyonder.co.uk*

| | | |
|---|---|---|
| Adults initiate the idea of the project | ←——→ | Young people initiate the idea of the project |
| Adults decide on agenda (on what is discussed) | ←——→ | Young people decide on agenda (on what is discussed) |
| Adults make decisions | ←——→ | Young people make decisions |
| Adults have most of the information necessary for decision making | ←——→ | Young people have most of the information necessary for decision making |
| Adults take actions to implement decisions | ←——→ | Young people take actions to implement decisions |
| Structure of participation replicates the adult way of doing things (rather formal) | ←——→ | Structure of participation replicates youth ways of doing things (rather informal) |
| **Adults have power** | **Power shared in between** | **Young people have power** |

| Participation snowball ||
|---|---|
| **Title** | **Participation snowball** |
| **Theme** | Defining participation<br>Participating in a decision-making process |
| **Sample** | Does youth participation mean the same to you as it does to me? |
| **Group size** | 8, 16 or 24 participants |
| **Time** | 60 minutes |
| **Objectives** | − to verbalise different understandings of youth participation;<br>− to reflect on different understandings, concepts and dimensions of youth participation;<br>− to reflect on participants' involvement in a decision-making process. |
| **Preparation** | None |
| **Materials** | Flipcharts, markers |

| | |
|---|---|
| **Instructions** | 1. Ask the participants to write down their definition of youth participation on a piece of paper (individual work).<br>2. Individuals find a partner and work in pairs. They each have to present their own definition and then have to agree on a common definition for both.<br>3. The pairs then form groups of four. Each pair presents its definition and then both pairs have to agree on a definition that will be acceptable for all four members of the group.<br>4. The groups of four now form groups of eight. All the definitions are presented and a final definition acceptable to everyone in the group has to be agreed on.<br>5. In the plenary discussion, each of the groups presents its definition, followed by time for comments and explanations.<br>6. Present some "official definitions" of youth participation to compare. |
| **Debriefing and evaluation** | Discussion about the results (definitions):<br>1. To what extent are the definitions of different groups similar?<br>2. What are the main differences?<br>3. To what aspects of youth participation do these definitions relate?<br>4. How difficult was it to come up with common definitions? Why?<br>5. To what extent were you ready to make concessions or to abandon parts of your definition in order to come up with a common agreement?<br>Debriefing of the decision-making process:<br>1. What was your role in formulating definitions at the different stages (in pairs, groups of four, etc.)? How did you feel about it?<br>2. Did you have as much space to participate as you wanted or needed? If not, why not?<br>3. What helped you to participate?<br>4. What hindered your participation?<br>5. How does the definition of participation presented in the plenary discussion relate to your participation experience from this exercise? |
| **Variations** | It might be interesting to have a few observers who would watch the process and then give feedback on how the different groups proceeded and what strategies they used. People are not necessarily aware of their own roles or their way of behaving. |

| Participation timeline ||
|---|---|
| Title | **Participation timeline**<br>Source: unknown |
| Theme | Introducing one's experience in youth participation |
| Sample | What's your story? |
| Group size | 4-25 |
| Time | 30-60 minutes |
| Objectives | − to share participants' experience in participation;<br>− to reflect on different ways in which individuals can participate in the life of some organisations or local communities;<br>− to create a basis for planning further involvement in the area of youth participation. |
| Preparation | None |
| Materials | A very big piece of paper, so that each participant has enough space to draw his time line<br>Lots of coloured pencils, markers, coloured paper, scissors, glue, tape, old magazine pictures, etc. |
| Instructions | 1. Using the materials available, the participants should draw a timeline showing the milestones that would present their most important experiences in the field of youth participation, for example:<br>   − how and when they participated in organisations, groups or communities;<br>   − how and when they were involved in strengthening or promoting youth participation.<br>2. Participants present their timelines and talk about their experiences in the field of youth participation. |
| Debriefing and evaluation | Ask participants the following questions:<br>1. What kind of participation experience is listed most often?<br>2. What are the factors that encourage young people, including yourself, to participate?<br>3. Now that you have seen everyone's timelines, are there elements of yours which you did not add but realise you could have?<br>4. Do all the listed elements seem participatory to you? How? |
| Tips for the facilitator | − ask participants to draw their timelines in such a way that they all meet at a central point on the paper (like sunrays, with the sun in the middle). This central point then represents your training event;<br>− if the group is bigger than 16 people, the drawings and presentations can be done in smaller groups. |
| Variations | The participation timeline can focus on more specific issues related to participation, such as specific forms of participation, specific levels (European, national, local), etc. |

| Rights and participation ||
|---|---|
| Title | **Rights and participation** |
| Theme | Rights related to youth participation |
| Sample | What are my rights? |
| Group size | 8 as a minimum |
| Time | 90 minutes |
| Objectives | – to review different rights that young people need to have in order to practice participation;<br>– to explore the relationship between young people's rights and participation;<br>– to reflect on how the rights of young people are respected in different local contexts. |
| Preparation | None |
| Materials | Flipchart and markers |
| Instructions | 1. Divide participants into groups of four to six people.<br>2. Ask each group to write down as many examples of rights related to participation as they can think of in five minutes (examples are the rights necessary for young people to participate in the life of their local community or region).<br>3. Collect the answers in a plenary discussion.<br>4. Ask each group to choose 10 rights from the plenary list that are, in their opinion, essential for meaningful youth participation in a local context.<br>5. Let the groups present their lists.<br>6. Invite everybody to a plenary discussion for a debriefing. |
| Debriefing and evaluation | Questions related to the results of the group work:<br>1. What are the similarities between the lists (what rights have been mentioned by all or the majority of groups)?<br>2. What rights do not appear on each list? Why not?<br>3. What criteria did you use to decide if a right is "essential" to participation or not?<br>4. How did your groups agree on these criteria?<br>Questions related to rights in general:<br>5. How do the rights listed by participants relate to youth participation?<br>6. Can these rights be considered to be human rights? Why?<br>Questions related to the local situations of participants:<br>7. What rights are not respected in your own local context? Why?<br>8. How can young people claim these rights? |

| | RMSOS charades |
|---|---|
| Title | **RMSOS charades**<br>Source: Training Course on the Development and Implementation of Participation Projects at Local and Regional Level, EYC Strasbourg, 2005 |
| Theme | Getting a first impression of the charter |
| Sample | What is RMSOS? |
| Group size | 15-30 |
| Time | 40 minutes |
| Objectives | – to reflect on concepts, scope and the different ways of understanding "youth participation";<br>– to analyse the relevance of different concepts of participation to participants' work and everyday life;<br>– to initiate a debate on young people's attitudes to participation. |
| Preparation | A simplified presentation of the charter should be given, namely what it is, what it was intended for and how it affects individuals. |
| Materials | Charter and youth-friendly version of Charter.<br>Flipchart. |
| Instructions | 1. Introduce the five elements of RMSOS:<br>   a. right;<br>   b. means;<br>   c. space;<br>   d. opportunities;<br>   e. support.<br>2. Ask participants to split into groups of three to six people. Each group is given one of the RMSOS concepts to discuss and they should then answer the following questions:<br>   a. What do you think this concept means?<br>   b. What are the consequences of this concept for participation?<br>3. Ask the groups to prepare a creative performance (a song, poem, sketch, drama, pantomime, ballet, etc.) presenting the main conclusions of their discussions.<br>4. Invite the groups to perform their creative piece.<br>5. Ask the rest of the participants to discover which of the RMSOS elements has been presented and how they interpret the poem, song, etc. |

| Debriefing and evaluation | In a plenary discussion, participants might be asked to go through each of the concepts and try to come up with a common understanding of what they mean in relation to the charter and to youth participation. |
|---|---|
| | You can also ask participants the following questions: |
| | 1. What did you learn about youth participation from this exercise? |
| | 2. How relevant is the RMSOS concept to your situation? |
| Variations | In order to make it more exciting, participants should have to guess which concept is being presented by the other group. This would also clarify how far they all interpret the concepts in similar ways. |

| Role play on the charter ||
|---|---|
| Title | **Role play on the charter** |
| | Source: Training Course on the Development and Implementation of Participation Projects at Local and Regional Level, EYC Strasbourg, 2005 |
| Theme | The charter in reality |
| Sample | Try the charter out in everyday life |
| Group size | 10+ |
| Time | 40 minutes |
| Objectives | – to show how situations can be modified by using the charter; |
| | – to experience different aspects of young people's lives where the charter can be used. |
| Preparation | None |
| Materials | Handouts describing the various roles |
| | Depending on participants' imagination, other materials might be needed |
| Instructions | 1. Form groups of four to five people. Explain to them that they will be acting out a specific situation. |
| | 2. Distribute roles to the different groups. |
| | 3. Ask them to look up what part of the charter is relevant to this specific situation. |
| | 4. Give the groups a few minutes to prepare their play. |
| | 5. Ask them to act out the situation in front of the others, using the revised charter to find a solution. |
| | 6. Invite the participants to share their views about the situations and solutions presented. |

| **Debriefing and evaluation** | Ask participants the following questions: <br> 1. What was the aim of this exercise? <br> 2. How can the charter be used as a tool here? <br> 3. How could you relate the sketches to your own personal situation? <br> 4. Was the exercise useful? Why? |
|---|---|
| **Variations** | In order to make the roles more lively, cartoons can be used to demonstrate the situations (see attached examples). |

### Role play on the charter – Handouts

*Housing*

The housing situation in Utopia is not good. There is far too little affordable housing available for young people. The municipality does not provide information about housing and is rather reluctant to provide housing services at all due to budget constraints. The team plays a group of young people demonstrating against the bad housing situation in Utopia, after having read the article on housing in the plain language version of the charter. A representative from the local authorities arrives and asks what all the fuss is about. The youth representative points out the relevant passage in the charter.

*Education*

The young people in Utopia have access to education and are asked for their opinions about class trips but they are not invited to comment on anything relating to the management of the school (this is an example of tokenism). Teachers and school authorities do not want to let go of power and argue that young people do not act responsibly enough to be taken seriously in the matter of the school's management. The school authorities even question young people's democratic right to get involved in such matters. An argument takes place between a pupil and a teacher. The pupil demands more rights for the student council. The teacher does not want to give away rights, insisting that young people are not ready to take responsibility. A local authority representative steps in with the relevant passage in the charter that supports the pupil's view.

*Media*

Young people in Utopia do have limited access to media, in particular print media, but have no access at all to television and radio. Even though the local TV station is run and owned by the municipality, they argue that young people are not professional enough and can not be trusted to deal with the expensive equipment. The team is sitting in the middle of a room watching TV, saying things like "why can't we influence this rubbish?" One member of a youth organisation says that his organisation will take this up with the local authority. The local authority responds that the media are there to cater for all generations, but that young people are not reliable enough to be given access to such equipment. The youth organisations point out the relevant passage in the charter, showing the importance for local authorities to provide support and training, etc.

*Youth parliament*

Utopia has had a youth parliament for two years and it has the right to approve proposals, which have to be acknowledged and replied to by the city council. The city council sees the youth parliament as a tool for getting first-hand information about the needs and wishes of young people living in the area. The team forms a youth parliament that sits in the inner circle of the city council's plenary meeting discussing anti-discrimination policies laid down in the charter. One representative presents this discussion to the mayor, who in turn offers some of the solutions proposed by the charter.

N.B. These are only examples. According to the group, you may want to use other sectorial policies and examples.

*Role play on the charter*

| | Statement exercise |
|---|---|
| **Title** | **Statement exercise** |
| **Theme** | Participation, dilemmas, roles and responsibilities |
| **Sample** | Decide, discuss and change your mind? |
| **Group size** | 10+ |
| **Time** | 60 minutes |
| **Objectives** | – to raise awareness of participants' own attitudes and limitations in working on issues of participation;<br>– to broaden participants' perspectives and approaches in dealing with youth participation;<br>– to use and develop discussion skills. |
| **Preparation** | The statements "I agree" and "I disagree" should be written on separate pages of a flipchart. A line needs to be drawn in the middle of the room to show the borderline between those who agree and those who disagree. |
| **Materials** | Statements on flipcharts (one per page), markers |
| **Instructions** | 1. Start with a brief introduction to participation of young people, the importance of collaboration between the various actors and the challenges of participation in day-to-day life.<br>2. Explain that you are now going to read a series of statements with which people may agree to a greater or lesser extent.<br>3. Point out the two extreme positions "I agree" and "I disagree". Ask people to position themselves on one side of the line. Those who do not know can position themselves in the middle.<br>4. Read out the statements one by one. After each statement, leave some time for people to position themselves.<br>5. Ask participants to explain why they have chosen their position and what their point of view is on the question. Explain that participants are allowed to change their position during the discussion. Try to leave time for everyone to discuss.<br>6. After a few minutes, read out the next statement.<br>7. When you have gone through all statements, bring the group back together for a debriefing. |

| | |
|---|---|
| **Debriefing and evaluation** | Ask participants the following questions:<br>1. How did you feel during this exercise?<br>2. Was it difficult to make a choice where to stand? Why?<br>3. What arguments were used? Those based on facts or on emotions?<br>4. Which were more effective?<br>5. Are there any comparisons between what people did and said during the exercise and what they do in reality?<br>6. Are the statements valid?<br>7. Was the exercise useful? Why? |
| **Tips for the facilitator** | The facilitator could put special emphasis on the following questions:<br>– How much do we actively listen to other people's arguments?<br>– How well do we make our point clear? How consistent are we in our opinions and ideas? |
| **Variations** | 1. In some cases, the exercise could be performed without allowing participants to talk. The statements could be purposely very provocative and participants would have to choose a side without discussing their opinions. In this case, during the debriefing, special attention should be drawn to the frustration of non-communication when giving an opinion.<br>2. Do not allow people to position themselves in the middle, make them take a stand. |
| **Suggestions for statements** | – young people are not interested in participation;<br>– young people participate only when they have problems;<br>– local authorities support youth participation when it is politically useful for them;<br>– some young people do not participate for cultural reasons;<br>– all young people have the right to participate;<br>– public authorities should be responsible for the financing and implementation of policies in support of youth participation;<br>– non-participation is a form of participation;<br>Statements can be chosen according to the objectives of the session and the context of the training |

| | The triangle of co-operation |
|---|---|
| **Title** | **The triangle of co-operation – Confusion city**<br>Source: *Training course on active youth participation*, EYC, Strasbourg, 2007. |
| **Theme** | Youth participation – co-operation between young people, youth NGOs and local governments |
| **Sample** | Exploring the different points of view and negotiate |
| **Group size** | 3-35 |
| **Time** | 90-120 minutes |
| **Objectives** | – to simulate negotiations between young people, youth NGOs and public authorities (decision makers);<br>– to outline the different needs of different actors;<br>– to share experiences from similar situations in participants' reality;<br>– to explore and promote fruitful communication and co-operation between the main actors. |
| **Preparation** | Case studies |
| **Materials** | Markers, A3 paper |
| **Instructions** | Participants are split up in three groups: the local authority, young people and representatives of a youth NGO. The group of young people can be bigger than the others if necessary. The following introduction is given to everyone:<br><br>"In the city of confusion the newly elected mayor wants to make a new 'social contract' between young people, youth NGOs and the local authorities. The reason is that the city is facing quite a few challenges and the mayor wants to involve the young people in public life and get the support of youth NGOs. Therefore he is asking for a meeting with young people and youth NGOs that are active in the city.<br><br>Your task is to formulate – from your group's perspective – what you would need in order to be able to solve the problem(s). Later on you will have the chance to present your needs to the other two actors. Your task is to negotiate with the two other actors until you find a common agreement on how to deal with the problem and who does what."<br><br>After the introduction one to three people from each group (depending on the group size in total) get the same challenge/problem. They have 10-15 minutes to discuss what they would need from the two other actors and to formulate two statements: one for each partner (for example, young people formulate one statement towards the NGOs and one statement towards the local authority). After that the people who have been working on the same challenge/problem meet and start negotiations. They have 45-60 minutes to come to an agreement. |

| Debriefing and evaluation | **Feelings** |
|---|---|
| | General? In the working groups on the case study? In the negotiations? |
| | **Process** |
| | – What happened in the groups? |
| | – Was it easy to prepare the statements in the small groups? Why (not)? |
| | – Was it easy to find an agreement with the two other actors, did you find any? Why did you succeed/fail? |
| | **Results** |
| | What do you think about the results? Do you agree with the outcomes? |
| | **Transfer to reality** |
| | – Is there any connection between the exercise and reality? If yes which one? |
| | – What did you learn from this exercise? What can you use/improve in your practice? |

*The triangle of co-operation – Case studies – Challenges/problems*

*Housing*

There is a huge housing problem in Confusion city, with only few free houses and very high renting costs. Many buildings belong to the municipality, most of them being quite old and needing proper renovation before someone could live in them. The municipality does not have much money to spend and applying to an European fund would take another two years before the money would be available.

*Educational*

The school curriculum is fixed by the national government. Young people are asking for alternative teaching methods and more space for extra-curricular activities. Specifically they are asking for more non-formal education methods. The local municipality manages the school together with the parents of the school students.

*Access to the media*

The only radio station transmits religious hymns half of the day and political discussions the rest of the day, with some music between 1 a.m. and 5 a.m. There are five people on the board of the radio station. The mayor, the only priest of the city, the political opponent of the mayor, the high-school director and the director of the local clinic.

*Cultural activities*

There are quite a lot of exchanges organised with other countries and cultural celebrations, but still there are many things missing such as intercultural events, excursions, trips and concerts with non-mainstream artists, including those from different countries. Apart from some NGOs it is the city's Departments of Cultural Affairs and Promotion of National Heritage that organise such events.

*Chances for employment*

The youth unemployment rate is quite high in confusion city and this causes a lot of frustration amongst young people. The very few jobs created were given to the previous mayor's friends and family. Young people do not have access to the job vacancies which are anyway only scarce and not enough for all of them.

*Information about health issues*

Awareness about health protection does not exist and people in a small society are really afraid to ask about subjects such as sexual reproduction and protection from sexually transmitted diseases. The only pharmacy in confusion city does not help by gossiping about who is buying what (condoms, pills, etc.).

*Youth policy*

There is a new national law for establishing local youth councils, the decisions of which have to be taken into consideration by the municipal council. Confusion city has the lowest rate of voting amongst young people and the new mayor believes that this shows a lack of political culture.

*Alcohol abuse*

Confusion city has the highest rate of alcohol-addicted young people in the region. This leads to fights every day and the bad health of young people. Immediate reaction is needed.

*Setting up a youth club*

In confusion city there is no youth club providing space for activities, Internet access and socialising and leisure time activities. There are only some local cafeterias where the young people hang around.

The case studies can be adapted according to the context and background of the group.

| \ | True or false? |
|---|---|
| **Title** | **True or false?** |
| **Theme** | Introducing the content of the charter |
| **Sample** | True or false? |
| **Group size** | Any |
| **Time** | 50 minutes |
| **Objectives** | – to review what participants know about the charter;<br>– to motivate participants to read the text of the charter;<br>– to highlight different issues addressed by the charter. |
| **Preparation** | A simplified presentation of the charter should be given: namely, what it is, what it was intended for and how it affects individuals. |
| **Materials** | Text of the charter<br>Copies of the true/false statements |
| **Instructions** | 1. Ask the participants to find out if the statements written on the handout are true or false (the participants are allowed to use the text of the charter).<br>2. When the time is up, the participants form groups of three, compare their answers and together agree on which statements are true and which not.<br>3. The answers provided by the groups are discussed in a plenary session. |
| **Debriefing and evaluation** | Ask participants the following questions:<br>1. What did you learn about the charter?<br>2. Which questions did you find the most challenging?<br>3. How did the decision-making process work in your small groups? What was your role? |
| **Variations** | A similar exercise can be created on the basis of the plain language version of the charter. |
| **Attached documents** | The statements handout |

## True or false statements about the revised charter

| Statement | True? | False? |
|---|---|---|
| The charter is addressed mainly to local authorities | | |
| The charter has the status of a convention | | |
| The charter has been revised by the Directorate of Youth and Sport of the Council of Europe | | |
| The charter defines who young people are | | |
| The charter applies to all young people without discrimination | | |
| According to the charter, youth participation means voting and standing for elections | | |
| In the field of health policy, local authorities are recommended to introduce counselling facilities for young people affected by tobacco, alcohol and drug problems | | |
| The charter contains recommendations for 15 different sectoral policies at local and regional levels | | |
| In a policy for sport and leisure, the charter recommends that local authorities finance yearly sports events for young people | | |
| The charter proposes that local employment opportunities for unemployed young people should be established | | |
| The charter obliges local authorities to provide all young people with free housing | | |
| The charter states that local authorities should provide support to youth organisations in rural areas | | |
| The charter recommends that priority should be given to young women over young men in the area of politics | | |
| The charter does not recognise environmental projects as being related to youth participation | | |
| The charter recommends that local authorities should support training in youth participation at a local level | | |
| The charter proposes that local authorities give free computers to young people to increase their participation | | |
| The charter demands that local authorities cover the costs of local youth projects | | |
| The charter recommends that youth councils should consist of young people who are members of organisations | | |
| The charter proposes the appointment of a guarantor at local level to defend young people's rights | | |

| What can you do for me? ||
|---|---|
| **Title** | What can you do for me? |
| **Theme** | Getting to know the content of the charter |
| | Co-operation between local authorities and youth organisations |
| **Sample** | How can local authorities support my work? |
| **Group size** | Minimum of 12 persons |
| **Time** | 40 minutes |
| **Objectives** | – to get to know the content of the charter; |
| | – to find out possible ways of using the charter in local situations; |
| | – to explore how different interest groups can use the charter; |
| | – to identify possible ways of approaching local authorities in addressing youth participation issues. |
| **Preparation** | The participants need to have a basic knowledge of the content of the charter. |
| **Materials** | Text of the charter |
| | Flipchart, markers |
| **Instructions** | 1. Explain that all the participants live and work in one local community in which the revised charter has just been introduced and that they represent different groups involved in youth participation work. |
| | 2. Ask them to join one of the interest groups: |
| |     a. members of the local youth volleyball club; |
| |     b. teachers of a local secondary school; |
| |     c. members of a local youth council; |
| |     d. youth living in a rural area; |
| |     e. an ethnic minority women's group; |
| |     f. peer group working on sex education. |
| | 3. Explain that each of the interest groups wants to use the charter to formulate some recommendations to local authorities so that youth participation in their own field can be strengthened. |
| | 4. Give 45 minutes for the small groups to go through the charter and formulate a maximum of seven recommendations to local authorities. |
| | 5. Invite the interest groups to present their recommendations. |
| | 6. Open the discussion for comments and remarks. |
| | 7. Open a discussion in the plenary session: "How can these types of recommendations be communicated to local authorities in the most efficient way?" The conclusions need to be recorded on a flipchart. |
| **Debriefing and evaluation** | Ask participants the following questions: |
| | 1. Was it easy to look at the charter from a point of view of the interest group that you belonged to? Why? |
| | 2. What new aspect of the charter did you learn about? |

| Variations | In order to give it an official touch, the facilitator could ask two to three participants (or team members) to play the role of local authority representatives who really listen to the recommendations and who make comments, criticisms or remarks. In this way the participants could identify more strongly with the group that they represent.
The reactions of local authority representatives can be discussed and the participants can then work on proposing strategies for better co-operation with local authorities. |
|---|---|

| Visit to Jeunessia ||
|---|---|
| Title | **Visit to Jeunessia** |
| Theme | Conditions for meaningful participation |
| Sample | Let's visit the perfect community of Jeunessia |
| Group size | 10-30 |
| Time | 150 minutes |
| Objectives | – to discuss some principles of participation;
– to look for ways of creating a space conducive to meaningful participation of young people at a local level;
– to reflect on how these measures can be used in participants' situations;
– to practice presentation skills. |
| Preparation | Divide the participants into groups of five |
| Materials | Flipcharts, pens, coloured paper, glue, etc. |
| Instructions | 1. Explain that each of the groups is a delegation that has just visited the community of Jeunessia, where they witnessed perfect conditions for youth participation. Now each group needs to share what they saw with the others.
2. Give the groups 45 minutes to prepare a visual presentation on the measures, actions, regulations and other ideas that have been successfully implemented in Jeunessia.
3. Invite the delegations to make a report of their visit.
4. Collect on the flipchart all the ideas about measures supporting youth participation at a local level.
5. Open the floor in the plenary session for any comments, views, etc.
6. Ask the participants to think individually about which of these measures could be implemented in their own community. |
| Debriefing and evaluation | Ask participants the following questions:
1. How did you feel when imagining your visit to Jeunessia, the perfect community for youth participation?
2. How realistic are the measures implemented there? (How realistic are the measures proposed and presented by the small groups?)
3. What was the quality of presentations made by the delegations? Could such a presentation be made for the mayor or community authorities or would it need some improvement? |
| Variations | The activity can focus more on the quality of presentations delivered by the delegations, as a presentation can be an important tool in winning allies and building partnerships at a local level. |

| | What happens if it doesn't happen? |
|---|---|
| **Title** | What happens if it doesn't happen? |
| **Theme** | Barriers to youth participation |
| **Sample** | What happens if it doesn't happen? |
| **Group size** | Any |
| **Time** | 90 minutes |
| **Objectives** | – to explore the barriers to participation;<br>– to understand the consequences of the lack of participation;<br>– to develop creativity. |
| **Preparation** | Divide participants into groups of 4-6 |
| **Materials** | Flipchart and markers |
| **Instructions** | 1. Small groups brainstorm on the possible consequences of non-participation of young people at a local level (namely, what happens if participation "doesn't happen"?).<br>2. The groups prepare a short play to illustrate one of the possible consequences.<br>3. Each of the groups presents the play to the others, who try to find out what it is exactly about. |
| **Debriefing and evaluation** | Ask participants the following questions:<br>1. Do any of the scenes that you have just seen remind you of a situation that you have experienced in your local community? Which one? What was the result?<br>2. What would be the factors or barriers blocking youth participation?<br>3. How can these be addressed in a local context? |
| **Variations** | – the performances/plays could take place in silence, so that the activity can focus more on the attitudes of participants;<br>– the performances of participants could take place in the form of a theatre forum. In such a case, the actors would need to replay the scene so that the other participants could interact and play one of the roles. In this way, all the performances would be interactive and would include ideas for possible solutions;<br>– the same activity can be used to explore the benefits of youth participation. |

| | Simulation exercise "Youth in action" |
|---|---|
| Title | **Simulation exercise "Youth in action"**<br>Source: Training Course on the Development and Implementation of Participation Projects at Local and Regional Level, EYC Strasbourg, 2005 |
| Theme | Simulation of the establishment of local co-operation between governmental and non-governmental sectors in the field of youth. This deals with the development of a local youth parliament, addressing topics such as participation, civil society, co-operation, decision making, representing interests and finding consensus, but also the dynamics of a meeting, chairing and running of a meeting and public speaking in general. |
| Sample | Let's start a youth council in our town! |
| Group size | 15-30 |
| Time | 20 minutes – Introduction to the exercise<br>120 minutes – Preparation and meeting simulation<br>60 minutes – Discussion and debriefing |
| Objectives | – to explore approaches to participation represented by different actors at a local level;<br>– to identify the interests of local stakeholders involved in supporting youth participation;<br>– to look for practical ways of establishing a participatory structure for young people at a local level;<br>– to train participants in decision making and consensus finding;<br>– to experience an official meeting for representing interests and exchanging points of view. |
| Preparation | Copying handouts |
| Materials | – a copy of the scenario for each participant;<br>– a personal role for each participant, prepared in advance with the names of participants;<br>– a sheet with role descriptions and questions for each observer (if applicable);<br>– a meeting room set up in a circle or square of tables and chairs; several smaller meeting rooms or spaces;<br>– paper and pens;<br>– a copy of all the role descriptions for each participant at the end of the simulation. |

Educational section

| | |
|---|---|
| **Instructions** | 1. Explain to the group that they will be guests in a city where the mayor wants to initiate the programme "Youth in action", aimed at establishing a local youth parliament.
2. Give the time frame of the simulation and the debriefing.
3. Distribute copies of the scenario to participants and give some time for them to read it carefully.
4. Distribute the individual roles and instruct participants not to show them to anyone. Allow some minutes for participants to imagine the person they are going to be during the simulation.
5. If there are observers, distribute the sheets with questions and give them some detailed instructions, if necessary. Ask the observers to sit at the back of the room. |
| **Debriefing and evaluation** | 1. Did you like the simulation?
2. What was your own role and how did you fulfil it?
3. At this point in the debriefing, the sheets with the descriptions of all the roles can be distributed. Alternatively, if time permits, participants could read aloud the role they were taking on during the simulation.
4. How were the decisions made?
5. What were the arguments that led to a decision?
6. Was the decision democratic? Did the process allow participation?
7. What were the impressions of the observers?
8. What would you do differently if you could run the meeting once again?
9. Was the meeting realistic? Could it have happened in reality?
10. Was the final outcome satisfactory in relation to the aim of enhancing participation and co-operation?
11. What have you learned/discovered during the exercise?
12. For trainers and group leaders: if you were to use this exercise in one of your programmes, when and for what objectives would you use it? |
| **Attached documents** | – the simulation game;
– the roles. |

## Simulation exercise "Youth in action"

### Scenario

Oldtown is a city in the state of Seniorland, a democratic country with no developed youth policy. While quite a few young people live in Oldtown and more than 20 youth organisations exist, youth has never played a very active role in the decision making of the community. After the elections fifteen months ago the new mayor, Ms Young, decided to become more proactive about involving young people. She announced the brand new programme "Youth in action", aimed at enhancing the participation of young people, as well as increasing and intensifying the co-operation between young people and the local authority. As part of this programme she wants to initiate the establishment of a local youth parliament.

In preparation for the setting up of this local youth parliament, the mayor is convening a consultative meeting involving different interest groups and partners to decide on the format and nature of the mayor's initiative.

The following persons participate in the meeting:

- the mayor, who is the chairperson of today's meeting (she is also the vice-president of the Committee of Local and Regional Authorities in Seniorland);
- the leader of the Oldtown's political opposition;
- the vice-president of the city parliament, who is also head of the Budget Committee;
- the headmaster of the local secondary school;
- the vice-president of the parents' association of the local school;
- the spokesman for the group "Senior volunteers for children";
- the priest of the local Catholic church;
- the coach of Oldtown's successful youth football team;
- a researcher from the Institute of Sociological Research at the University of Oldtown;
- a board member of an international non-governmental youth organisation;
- the president of Oldtown's youth council;
- the secretary general of a minority youth organisation;
- a member of one of Oldtown's youth organisations;
- the community youth worker;
- the community development officer;
- the CEO of a local business company and four young people.

### Today's meeting discusses the following questions

- Is the establishment of a local youth parliament wanted and needed?
- If so, what format should it take?
- What should be the mandate of a local youth parliament?

## ⇢ Simulation exercise "Youth in action"

### *Role descriptions*

Your personal role description.

Please read it very carefully and do not show it to anyone.

Try to imagine how this person would act.

### *You are the mayor of Oldtown*

You won last year's election by a landslide, defeating the long-governing SPP (Senior People's Party) and the former mayor. One of the reasons you won the election is the emphasis of your electoral campaign on young people and youth policy. You are determined to do something to improve the situation of young people, their participation in society and the co-operation between your administration and youth. A few weeks ago, you presented your brand new programme "Youth in action", aimed at enhancing the participation of young people, as well as increasing and intensifying the co-operation between young people and the local authority. As part of this programme you want to initiate the establishment of a local youth parliament. In preparation for the setting up of this local youth parliament, you are convening a consultative meeting involving different interest groups and partners. You hope that this meeting will be positive and constructive, because while you like the idea of a youth parliament, you do not have much information about how it should work and how it could be set up. You are very enthusiastic and you want to show it.

### *You are a 55-year-old member of the opposition party*

You have lived all your life in the town, have been a member of the party for twenty-five years and you are the former mayor. You believe that young people should join a political party if they want to participate and you do not see a need for any youth representative structure. Therefore, you are against the mayor's idea and you try to derail it.

### *You are the vice-president of the city parliament*

You are also head of the Municipal Budget Committee. You have been working for years to achieve a balanced budget and finally succeeded last year. You want to keep a budget surplus by any means possible. Nevertheless, you are on good terms with the mayor. You support her initiative rather reluctantly. You would not mind if the initiative did not happen.

### *You are the headmaster of the local school*

Most of the young people who would be affected by the proposed youth parliament attend your school. They already have the opportunity to participate in the democratic running and management of the school through class representatives. You are concerned that this youth parliament will take attention and particularly financial resources away from the extra-curricular and leisure activities already offered at the school. Overall, you think that the money would be better invested in the renovation of the school sport facilities and do not really see the point of the initiative. You are also worried that the mayor has proposed this initiative in order to win approval of the international NGO active in the local area and that it is, in fact, a publicity stunt. You do not believe the mayor is really interested in promoting youth participation. You are against this initiative and forcefully argue your case.

### *You are the concerned parent of one of the school children*

You are an active member and the vice-president of the parents' association at the local school. You have invested a lot of time and energy in supporting the school class representatives and the school board. You believe in the established system and the participation of the class representatives in the school decision-making process. Most young people go to the school, and therefore you see the initiative as something of a waste of time and a duplication of effort. You are worried that it will cause unnecessary competition with the school democracy you are working for. You are against this initiative.

### *You are the parent of one of the young people*

You take part in the extra-curricular activities run by the school. You are also the spokesperson of an initiative called "Senior volunteers for children". From time to time, the headmaster asks you to come to the school to help out and supervise the extra-curricular activities. You do this with pleasure, but find it difficult to simply watch over the activities and supervise, as often you feel forced to get involved because the young people are badly behaved and are not able to manage their tasks by themselves. You are concerned that the extra-curricular activities you are involved in will lose out (in numbers) to the proposed youth parliament. You also doubt whether any initiative proposing to give so much responsibility to the young people can really work. You are sceptical about this whole initiative.

### *You are the local parish priest*

You are becoming increasingly concerned with the fact that the local youth are not interested in coming to the church or the parish activities. You are happy to have been invited to this meeting, as several young people and the representatives of youth organisations will be present, and you are interested in finding out from them what interests young people. You basically support this initiative, as young people increasingly turn away from God, and anything that will encourage young people to be more interested in getting involved in community life will be good for your parish activities.

### *You are the coach of the school football team*

You are a very active and dynamic person who likes to see young people getting involved and taking initiatives and responsibility for the things they are interested in and the issues that concern them. However, your football team has been suffering from a lack of financial support and you agree with the headmaster that perhaps the money would be better invested in the school sport facilities, as they seem to be the activities in highest demand by the local young people. You have a dilemma. You support any initiative to promote youth participation, but you are concerned about the competition that the parliament will create for financial resources.

### *You are a researcher in the Institute of Sociological Research at Oldtown University*

At the moment, your main subject of research is citizenship studies, but your real passion is youth research. This initiative has taken you by surprise and you are motivated to be involved because one of your main areas of interest is modes of participation of young people in local decision and policy making. You have plenty of advice to offer to the meeting concerning "participatory" approaches to consultation and policy making, having recently been to an international conference on this subject organised by the Council of Europe in Strasbourg. At the conference, youth parliaments were congratulated as examples of good participation practice, especially when young people themselves are involved in setting them up from the beginning. You are in favour of this initiative and provide "evidence-based" arguments from your own research to forcefully argue your case.

### *You represent an international students' NGO*

Your NGO deals with educational policies, advocating students' rights and organising international youth exchanges. You believe in the mayor's idea as something that will bring real and positive change in the local community. You are convinced that the initiative will be successful because all other democratic countries have local structures to help represent youth opinion and to solve important questions together with local authorities. Oldtown did not have any serious working structure until now (there is a local youth council, but this just unites several small organisations and is dilettante in encouraging youth).

### *You are the president of the local youth council*

Your youth council was established ages ago and has been functioning effectively. All youth organisations are satisfied with your activities and your work. You think that the mayor's idea is not relevant to Oldtown, because the youth council that you represent already does all that the youth parliament would do. You are strongly against the idea and believe that youth organisations and youth in general do not need youth parliaments. You believe they are elitist and not representative and that they therefore have no legitimacy. As a shadow structure, they have no decision-making power and they are constantly abused by politicians who use them to justify their unpopular decisions. You also believe from your own experience that a youth parliament is far too large a structure to be effective and efficient and you therefore strongly argue against the initiative.

### *You represent the local minority youth organisation*

Your organisation unites three national minorities living in the town. The activities of your organisation are extremely important because you help to sustain cultures and traditions. Your organisation represents minority youth to local authorities as well as to other organisations and structures. You have established good relations with the municipality and your organisation has been working with them on several common projects. You do not have much against the mayor's idea, but you want to make absolutely sure that the youth parliament will truly represent the young people of Oldtown, including its minorities. You therefore try to convince the mayor that there should be a quota ensuring the participation of minority youth.

### *You are a member of the local youth club*

Your club has sent you to this meeting to get more information about the mayor's idea. You generally like the idea of the youth parliament, but you want to make sure that your club will play an important role in establishing and running the parliament because you are the biggest youth club in your town.

### *You graduated last year with a degree in youth work*

You are enthusiastic and motivated to support young people in every way you can. You support the mayor's initiative but you are fearful that the mayor is using this initiative for her own political aims. Of course, you cannot express this directly in the meeting, but you want to make sure that the initiative brings about a sustainable structure for youth participation. Whenever you can, you ask questions along these lines, making sure that this whole thing will be more than a publicity stunt.

### *You have been working with different communities in the town for about seven years*

You generally work well together with the youth worker, but you are worried that the mayor's initiative will shift the focus away from your work more towards the work of your colleague. You officially support the mayor's initiative while privately you are not keen on seeing it happen. In the meeting, you try to point out the added value and impact of inter-generational work for the development of the community.

### *You own a local business*

You are constantly on the lookout for new business opportunities. You would like to become a friend of the mayor because you believe that this might generate some business for you. You, therefore, fully support the mayor's initiative. You would be willing to support it financially under certain conditions.

### *You are the best student in your school*

You have been sent to this meeting by one of your teachers. You do not understand what is going on during the meeting, but you are really keen to understand. Consequently, you keep asking people to explain what they really mean and what the things mean that you have not understood. The more you ask, the better!

### *You are 17 years old and you are interested in local politics*

You see many initiatives that have been undertaken in your local community for the benefit of young people that have been unsuccessful (due to little or no commitment from local authorities and young people themselves). The new initiative of the mayor is, in your opinion, the next failed initiative in this community. You would like to prevent this initiative from happening altogether because you find it pointless, which you make very clear whenever you can during the meeting.

### *You are fed up with your family*

You are also fed up with the school and especially the authorities (any authorities: local ones, the government and the whole lot). You are convinced that they should just stop bothering young people and give them freedom. You think that this youth parliament is another "genius" idea of the local authorities so that they can control young people. And what you want is freedom! You do not want to get involved in anything that has any link with local authorities, but you decided to join the meeting to have a chance to tell this crazy mayor what you think: that young people need space for participation without having a controlling structure forced onto them.

### *You are 16 years old*

Your friend from Youngtown has told you how wonderfully their youth parliament works. When you read about the mayor's idea in the newspaper you got really excited. You find the idea fantastic, and you want to support it and the mayor wherever you can. You also would like to get involved yourself, of course.

# Bibliography

*Advocacy kit*, Advocates for Youth, Washington, DC, n.d.

Boukobza, E., *Keys to participation. A practitioners' guide*, Council of Europe, 1998.

*Co-management. A practical guide. Seeking excellence in youth participation at a local level*, Peace Child International, 2006.

*Discussing global issues: what is participation?* UNICEF, United Kingdom, 2004.

Doorley, J., "Synthesis report on the work of the Council of Europe's Directorate of Youth and Sport in the field of youth participation and democratic citizenship between 2003 and 2005 and an analysis of current trends in youth participation and recommendations for future action", CDEJ(2006)4, Strasbourg, 2006.

Dussap, A. and Merry, P., (eds), "Project management T-kit", Council of Europe and European Commission, 2000.

Forbrig, J. (ed.), *Revisiting youth political participation*, Council of Europe, 2005.

Golombek, S. (ed.), *What works in youth participation: case studies from around the world*, International Youth Foundation, 2002.

Hart, R. A., *Children's participation from tokenism to citizenship*, UNICEF Innocenti Research Centre, Florence, 1992.

Jans, M. and De Backer, K., *Youth(work) and social participation. Elements for a practical theory*, Flemish Youth Council JeP!, Brussels, 2002.

Kirby, P. and Bryson, S., *Measuring the magic? Evaluating and researching young people's participation in public decision-making*, Carnegie Young People Initiative, London, 2002.

Kovacheva, S., *Keys to youth participation in eastern Europe*, Council of Europe, 2000.

Lauritzen, P., "Essentials of a youth policy in the Council of Europe", unpublished paper, 2006.

Marx, M., Finger, W. and Mahler, H. (eds), *Youth participation guide: assessment, planning, and implementation*, Family Health International, 2005.

McAuley, K. and Brattman, M., *Hearing young voices. Executive summary*, Open Your Eyes to Child Poverty Initiative, Ireland, 2002.

McGachie, C. and Smith, K., *Youth participation case studies*, Ministry of Youth Affairs, New Zealand, 2003.

*Networking for policy change. An advocacy training manual*, The Policy Project, 1999.

*People & participation. How to put citizens at the heart of decision-making*, Involve, 2005.

Torjman, S., *What is policy?*, Caledon Institute of Social Policy, 2005.

Weafer, J., (prep.) and Woods, M. (ed.), "Jigsaw of advocacy", *COMHAIRLE, 2003*.

*Young voices. Guidelines on how to involve children and young people in your work*, The National Children's Office, Ireland, 2005.

*Youth participation handbook for organisations. A guide for organisations seeking to involve young people on boards and committees*, Government of South Australia Office for Youth, 2003.

*Youth policy formulation manual*, United Nations, New York, 1999.

# Contacts

**Directorate of Youth and Sport**
**European Youth Centre Strasbourg**
30, rue Pierre de Coubertin
F-67000 Strasbourg
Tel.: +33 (0)3 88 41 23 00
Fax: +33 (0)3 88 41 27 77/78
e-mail: youth@coe.int
www.coe.int/youth

**European Youth Foundation**
30, rue Pierre de Coubertin
F-67000 Strasbourg
Tel.: +33 (0)3 88 41 20 19
Fax: +33 (0)3 90 21 49 64
e-mail: eyf@coe.int

**European Youth Centre Budapest**
Zivatar utca 1-3
H-1024 Budapest
Tel.: +36 1 438 10 60
Fax: +36 1 213 40 76
e-mail: eycb.secretariat@coe.int
www.eycb.coe.int

**Congress of Local and Regional Authorities of the Council of Europe**
Council of Europe
F-67075 Strasbourg Cedex
Tel.: +33 (0)3 88 41 21 10
Fax: +33 (0)3 88 41 27 51
e-mail: congress.web@coe.int

# Sales agents for publications of the Council of Europe
# Agents de vente des publications du Conseil de l'Europe

**BELGIUM/BELGIQUE**
La Librairie Européenne -
The European Bookshop
Rue de l'Orme, 1
BE-1040 BRUXELLES
Tel.: + 32 (0)2 231 04 35
Fax: + 32 (0)2 735 08 60
E-mail: info@libeurop.eu
http://www.libeurop.be

Jean De Lannoy/DL Services
c/o Michot Warehouses
Bergense steenweg 77
Chaussée de Mons
BE-1600 SINT PIETERS LEEUW
Fax: + 32 (0)2 706 52 27
E-mail: jean.de.lannoy@dl-servi.com
http://www.jean-de-lannoy.be

**CANADA**
Renouf Publishing Co. Ltd.
22-1010 Polytek Street
CDN-OTTAWA, ONT K1J 9J1
Tel.: + 1 613 745 2665
Fax: + 1 613 745 7660
Toll-Free Tel.: (866) 767-6766
E-mail: order.dept@renoufbooks.com
http://www.renoufbooks.com

**CROATIA/CROATIE**
Robert's Plus d.o.o.
Marasoviçeva 67
HR-21000 SPLIT
Tel.: + 385 21 315 800, 801, 802, 803
Fax: + 385 21 315 804
E-mail: robertsplus@robertsplus.hr

**CZECH REPUBLIC/
RÉPUBLIQUE TCHÈQUE**
Suweco CZ, s.r.o.
Klecakova 347
CZ-180 21 PRAHA 9
Tel.: + 420 2 424 59 204
Fax: + 420 2 848 21 646
E-mail: import@suweco.cz
http://www.suweco.cz

**DENMARK/DANEMARK**
GAD
Vimmelskaftet 32
DK-1161 KØBENHAVN K
Tel.: + 45 77 66 60 00
Fax: + 45 77 66 60 01
E-mail: reception@gad.dk
http://www.gad.dk

**FINLAND/FINLANDE**
Akateeminen Kirjakauppa
PO Box 128
Keskuskatu 1
FI-00100 HELSINKI
Tel.: + 358 (0)9 121 4430
Fax: + 358 (0)9 121 4242
E-mail: akatilaus@akateeminen.com
http://www.akateeminen.com

**FRANCE**
Please contact directly /
Merci de contacter directement
Council of Europe Publishing
Éditions du Conseil de l'Europe
F-67075 STRASBOURG Cedex
Tel.: + 33 (0)3 88 41 25 81
Fax: + 33 (0)3 88 41 39 10
E-mail: publishing@coe.int
http://book.coe.int

Librairie Kléber
1, rue des Francs-Bourgeois
F-67000 STRASBOURG
Tel.: + 33 (0)3 88 15 78 88
Fax: + 33 (0)3 88 15 78 80
E-mail: librairie-kleber@coe.int
http://www.librairie-kleber.com

**NORWAY/NORVÈGE**
Akademika
Postboks 84 Blindern
NO-0314 OSLO
Tel.: + 47 2 218 8100
Fax: + 47 2 218 8103
E-mail: support@akademika.no
http://www.akademika.no

**POLAND/POLOGNE**
Ars Polona JSC
25 Obrowncow Street
PL-03-933 WARSZAWA
Tel.: + 48 (0)22 509 86 00
Fax: + 48 (0)22 509 86 10
E-mail: arspolona@arspolona.com.pl
http://www.arspolona.com.pl

**PORTUGAL**
Marka Lda
Rua dos Correeiros 61-3
PT-1100-162 LISBOA
Tel: 351 21 3224040
Fax: 351 21 3224044
E mail: apoio.clientes@marka.pt
www.marka.pt

**RUSSIAN FEDERATION/
FÉDÉRATION DE RUSSIE**
Ves Mir
17b, Butlerova ul. - Office 338
RU-117342 MOSCOW
Tel.: + 7 495 739 0971
Fax: + 7 495 739 0971
E-mail: orders@vesmirbooks.ru
http://www.vesmirbooks.ru

**SWITZERLAND/SUISSE**
Planetis Sàrl
16, chemin des Pins
CH-1273 ARZIER
Tel.: + 41 22 366 51 77
Fax: + 41 22 366 51 78
E-mail: info@planetis.ch

**TAIWAN**
Tycoon Information Inc.
5th Floor, No. 500, Chang-Chun Road
Taipei, Taiwan
Tel.: 886-2-8712 8886
Fax: 886-2-8712 4747, 8712 4777
E-mail: info@tycoon-info.com.tw
orders@tycoon-info.com.tw

**UNITED KINGDOM/ROYAUME-UNI**
The Stationery Office Ltd
PO Box 29
GB-NORWICH NR3 1GN
Tel.: + 44 (0)870 600 5522
Fax: + 44 (0)870 600 5533
E-mail: book.enquiries@tso.co.uk
http://www.tsoshop.co.uk

**UNITED STATES and CANADA/
ÉTATS-UNIS et CANADA**
Manhattan Publishing Co
670 White Plains Road
USA-10583 SCARSDALE, NY
Tel: + 1 914 472 4650
Fax: + 1 914 472 4316
E-mail: coe@manhattanpublishing.com
http://www.manhattanpublishing.com